Home Buying, Everything You _Must_ Know

Second Edition

Paul E. Hunt, Esq.

By Paul E. Hunt, Esq.
Direct inquires to:
PEHBooks@aol.com

ISBN-10: 1460900596

ISBN-13: 978-1460900598

Dedicated to <u>you</u>,
with my genuine hope
that you find the personal
satisfaction of self-directed
investment and the financial
security it brings.

Table of Contents

Understanding Property

10. Credit
How They FICO Calculated
Improving Credit Scores
        Add A Child
        Moving Debt
        Keep Old Accounts
        Get More Credit Cards
        Debt Reorganization Companies
        Fixing Incorrect Data

11. Financing
Loan Terms
        Mortgages And Trust Deeds
        Point
        Fixed Rate
        ARM (Adjustable Rate Mortgage)
        Amortized
        Negative Amortization
        Balloon
        Direct Lender
        Prepayment Penalty
        PMI
        FI Requirements
        Income
        Aging Reserves
        Employment
        No Or Low Docs
        Interest Rate

12. Creative Financing
        Hard Money
        Co-signer
        "Strawman"
        "Double Dipping"
        "Buy And Refi"
        Credit Cards
        Seller's Adjustments
        Seller Carry Back
        Inflated Appraisals
        Phony Paperwork?

Foreword

People usually read the forward to find out why they should buy a book. The answer this time is simple: if you want to know how to make money in real estate and learn the tricks and inside information that most people don't know, then buy this book!

Still haven't decided to buy it? I know your time has value, so I will make this to the point.

Most books I have read on real estate either repeat the same basic information and unrealistic claims or cram in facts like a college course. I have taken a different angle. I explain the concepts simply and in a friendly manner, as if we were having a chat over coffee. I talk about how to do transactions as if I were sitting beside you, looking over your paperwork. I believe people better understand information when they know not just the answer, but why the answer is what it is. This allows you to move beyond what I tell you and evaluate situations for yourself.

Prior homeowners and investors with 5 or 10 properties under their belts may know, for example, what escrow is, but probably do not know all the inner workings of a transaction or how they can save money by knowing more. There are opportunists looking to deceive you, and you will want to know how to spot them. We will go over the common dishonest scams and how to avoid them. Part of what you must know is what will not work.

It is best to keep an optimistic outlook, but I will also tell you about the downsides and the hard work. If you were about to take a job with the post office, you would want to know how many biting dogs would be on your route; I will therefore be up-front with you about the potential pitfalls. There is a lot of money to be made in real estate, and someone else is making it right now. Jump in and take your share, knowing there are always hurdles to overcome before you achieve any accomplishment.

You will gain more from this book than from other books because I will help you understand the fundamentals that affect all aspects of your investment without repeating myself or going into more of the trivial details than you need. Nothing is better than experience, and with me walking you through the way real-life transactions take place, you will have the benefit of learning from mine.

I am not going to waste your time and mine by saying fluffy things I have seen in other books like "If you are thinking of having another baby, you may want a larger home" or "You may want to be close to a school"; I would like to assume you know your personal needs and desires. Some readers may take issue with my assertion that buyers looking for homes for their families should think about the eventual sales prices and how improvements may add to the value. Remember, however, that the average first-time buyer sells his home in about nine years. Whenever you end up selling, you will be very thankful to have purchased with an eye towards increased value. Even your "dream home" is an investment, and this book is about looking at real estate as an investment for the highest short-term or long-term benefit.

Property is unique from location to location, and the prices can be very different. I will pick easy-to-work-with numbers. Most of my example homes will be in the range of $500,000, but the same math will give you the same percent profit whether you live in an area of $50,000 homes or $5,000,000 homes. I will use 7% or 8% interest in my examples; if the current rate is less, your profit will be better. I would rather err on the side of understating the potential profits of these investments than mislead homebuyers about what they can expect to earn. If a deal works in the worst-case economic situation, it will generally also work under more favorable circumstances. I will need to use math to show how some deals work. If math is not your thing, feel free to skim those parts, since I will also be telling you why the result is good or bad.

I need to add a little disclaimer. As a wise investor, you should double-check any book you read as to which laws and procedures are currently being used in your area. They can change over time and are often very different from place to place.

I truly hope you get the most value possible from your efforts and thrive in the power of self-directed control of your investments.

Now buy the book!

Understanding Property

In any job, industry, or even in some social clubs, you will need to take time to understand the terms, concepts, and ways things work before you can become a leader in that area. An elderly friend once told me a story. In his youth, he was trying to get a job on a steam ship and there was an opening in the "pantry." He told the captain he was a good "painter" because he had never heard the work "pantry" before. The same thing can happen in real estate. People have spent lifetimes learning just one aspect of this very complicated topic. You as a buyer do not need to know everything, but you need to know what will affect you and how to secure the best possible deal. If the agent says the seller will consider a "land contract," you should know whether this is something good or bad.

In this section we will go over the basics. Even if you have bought and sold several properties in the past and know some of the terminology, you may lack a full understanding of how and why things work and how to better use this information.

We will go over the value of money and how investments work for you, what property rights are, what you will own, the people you will deal with, and the functions of their jobs. We will then walk though a transaction as I describe what is really going on behind the scenes. The reason you need to know this is that knowledge is power. You will understand and be able to speak the lingo, and you will know what to expect as you negotiate and control your transactions.

1.   Real Estate as an Investment

Everyone is reading this book for the same reason: *money*. Whether you want to make money, control the money you have to make more money, or retain your money value against inflation, you have figured out that real estate may be the best way.

If we could add up the value of all the bank accounts, gold, cars and other valuables in the United States and compare them with the value of all the land in the country, we would find that most of this nation's (and the world's) value is in the land we are living on. More money has been made in real estate than in any other investment!

Other Investments
All things of value have ups and downs in their prices, but real estate is the most reliable and safest investment in the long term, with a relatively steady 8% return on value. Let's talk about the other well-known investments first, as I demonstrate the concepts behind investing. Before we look at them, remember that the inflation rate for the last 50 years has been, on average, 3.5% per year. This means that products cost you that much more each year. In other words, if new car tires cost $100 this year and you only make 2% interest on the money in your savings account, your $100 will be $102 next year, but you've lost buying power because the tires will cost $103.50. If you only make 3.5% on your money, you have not increased your buying power, but if you make 5% on your money, then you will have $105.00 and can buy those tires next year and have money left over. In order to add to your wealth, you must beat the rate of inflation.

People like the idea of being millionaires, but the buying power of a million dollars has changed over time. Let's assume someone had a million dollars in 1960. How rich was that person in buying power then, compared to a person with a million dollars 50 years later? To figure this out, we look at the inflation rate of 3.5%. Using this math, we find that a person in the year 2010 would have needed $5,585,000 to have the same buying power as someone with $1,000,000 in 1960. Another way of looking at this is that a person in the year 2010 with $1,000,000 has the same buying power as someone in 1960 with only $179,000.

(Note: The Consumer Price Index "CPI" is the accepted method to calculate inflation; other factors exist concerning the quality of goods sold. For this reason, and to keep the math easier, this book uses the rule of thumb of 3.5% yearly. The actual average CPI between 1960 and 2010 was 4.075%, which would exaggerate the $5,585,000 to $7,366,756 and reduce the $179,000 to $135,744. Thus, per government statistics, someone with $135,744 in 1960 had the buying power of a 2010 millionaire.)

With the inflation rate in mind, let's look at investments:

Stocks – Owning a piece of a company is only as valuable as what someone is willing to pay you for your piece of that company. Sure, there are people who make money in stocks, just as there are people who have made money gambling; you just don't hear them brag about all the times they lost before they won. Figure that the real people who make big money are those guys that fly their jet-powered helicopters to work at the stock exchange. They have a lot more knowledge about the inner workings of the companies than even the most educated stock investor. Any company can financially go under, whether it is through mismanagement, economic changes, major lawsuits, or outright corporate theft by management. Let's use Enron as an example: the stock dropped from $90 per share to 25 cents. In stocks, it is possible to lose virtually all the money you've invested.

Today as I write this, the news is announcing another all-time high for the Dow Jones Average. There are innumerable ways to measure the stock market, but the Dow is the most common, and today it is the highest in all history. Surely that's a great reason to invest in the stock market, right? Ten years ago, the Dow was relatively stable and about half of what it is today. Looks great: it doubled!

But if we look at my handy-dandy interest rate calculator, an investor ten years ago would have made an average of 7.18% on his money per year. "Good," you may say, "this is double the inflation rate." But things have been good over the last ten years. I could show you a different 10-year span where an investor could have lost 25% of his money based on the Dow. Furthermore, the Dow was historically based on 30 companies in the "industrial industries," nowadays "corporate industry," which have been chosen for their strength and growth. When they get weak, they are replaced, so the eventual downfall of that company is not calculated within the Dow. Using a more complete indicator like the Wilshire 5000, you will find the average stock profits are closer to the inflation rate (yields including dividends not included). You should further understand that this is an average, and most of that profit was made by the really big investors, while most of the losses were taken by the day traders.

Bonds – A bond is an "I owe you" from a company or government agency. Just as with stocks, the company may not be able to pay back the debt if it goes under. Think about it for a minute: companies that need to borrow your money don't have the money they need to operate. Those companies believe that they will make much more on your money and will be able to pay you back some of the profit they make. Those companies decide how much interest they are willing to pay. If a company believes it is a safe bet for you, it will offer as little interest as it can. The companies that pay higher interest do so because people have deemed them bad risks, and so they need larger incentives. Government bonds are more secure because it is unlikely that a city, state, or the federal government will be unable to pay back their IOU. However, they know how secure they are and may pay under the inflation rate. If the inflation rate goes up faster than the profit on your money, you will have less spending power when you get your money back.

Gold – Gold has been the universal symbol of wealth since humans noticed it was shinier than seashells. In the last several years, the price for gold has doubled, making the investment look pretty secure. But the history of gold prices in America shows a different story. Starting our investigation during the 139 years when the United States still backed the dollar with gold (1793 to 1932), the price only rose from $19.39 to $20.67. For the next 30 years (until 1963) it only went up to $35.50, equal to 1.8 % per year. The best time to have bought gold was in 1970 when it was $39, then to have been lucky enough to sell it at its all-time high of $850 in 1980, equal to 36.0 % per year growth. However, if you bought in 1980, you would have lost two thirds of your money over the next 20 years (2000) as it dropped to $264. Ten years later, in 2010, it jumped up to around $1,300. This becomes less impressive, however, when you adjust for inflation and discover it would need to have been $2,300 to match the buying power it had in 1980. Only by cherry-picking your dates can gold look like it has been profitable. Gold's value changes greatly and unpredictably. Its long-term average is very low and under the inflation rate.

There must be one commercial on TV an hour with some "expert" wanting to sell you his gold. Ever think about why someone would advise you to buy something he is trying to sell? Some say that if there is ever a catastrophic event, paper money will be useless and only gold bars will still buy you a can of beans. I would argue that buying a case of canned beans in advance might be a better investment for that disaster, and a lot cheaper. Should that disaster occur, you could sell your cans of beans for other people's bars of gold.

If and when, in our scientific world, someone invents a way to amass more gold than we currently have available, the value of gold will plummet. This may sound like the pipe dreams of alchemists, but it is not impossible. There is gold floating in the oceans of the world (0.1 to 2 mg/ton), and a nuclear reactor has created gold. At the moment these processes cost more than the value of the gold they produce, but if someone ever finds an inexpensive way to make or harvest gold, it could become more worthless than seashells.

Collectables – It is fun to buy plates, art, stamps, coins, and even cars to hide away and wait until someone will pay you more for them than you paid. But remember, the people who sell these know you are investing and inflate their prices accordingly. On the TV shopping channel, you can find some company selling a "limited number" of commemorative plates for $49.99 each. If you buy them, you must hope they go up in value: some do, some don't. The next problem is when do you sell them? If you have held a commemorative plate for 25 years, are you really ever going to sell it at all?

Let's look at one of the best-known examples of a lucrative collectable: Superman one, issue one, first edition. It went on sale in 1939 for $0.10 and is worth about half a million at auction today. Sounds great, but someone waited over 70 years on a long shot. Remember, this is the extreme case, and few collectables can brag about this type of return. Checking eBay today, I found many other comic books of the same year priced under a dollar and receiving no bids. If a person had purchased all possible collectables in 1939, kept them in perfect unused condition for 70 years, and sold them all, the average increase per year would be about 1%. No one knows what will someday have value. Besides, collectables only have high prices when the economy is good: few will pay much for your comic book when they can't pay their rent.

Are the above investments bad?
People have made money on all kinds of investments, but many investments are high risk and low profit for all but the luckiest investors. If you are trying to make your fortune, this is a long shot.

If you have already made your retirement money, staggered levels of diversification is great to protect against short-term losses. It takes little work to check your stock reports, keep a safety deposit box, or dust off your collectables. Those investments give you something little with little work. However, even if you have those types of investments, you still need some form of reliable, long-term source of income to balance out the possible low return on your other investments.

Now let's look at real estate!
It was best said by cowboy movie star, Will Rogers (1879 - 1935): "Buy land. They ain't making any more of the stuff." A very true statement! As long as there are people and their numbers are growing, we will need land to live on and for the production of food and goods. Real estate increases in value because of a never-ending demand, and its owners profit accordingly. Although it does fluctuate somewhat in price with the changing economy, it never becomes worthless as other investments can. You can easily control five times more property than the money you've invested through leverage. Other factors, such as tax benefits and rental income, add to the profit. Real estate wins as the best and safest investment!

Any modern discussion of the safety of real estate investment must address the "crash" which began in 2006 and caused home prices to drop considerably. This caused a lot of hardship, as the average home price dropped from $240,000 to about $160,000 in 2 years. Looking at the short-term trend, that sounds terrible. But if you look further back, in 2000 the average home price was $125,000. Because of overly relaxed loan programs, anyone could qualify for a loan, and the average home price nearly doubled in just 6 years. The theory of "supply and demand" states that when there is more demand than supply, the price goes up. There were a limited number of homes, and almost everyone who applied qualified to buy one. When many of the people who had purchased overpriced homes that they should not have qualified for could not make their payments, the price of homes dropped back to what a qualified buyer could spend. The demand dropped to normal, and the prices started to even out. The average price returned to what it had been in 2004, and so anyone who had bought before 2004 still experienced an overall increase in property value during and after the "crash." By the end of 2010, the price of a home had readjusted to what it should have been based on a 40-year growth pattern. In short, the price inflated because of outside circumstances but returned to the same predictable growth pattern.

During the artificial excessive price increase of 2004, I was running a loan company. I kept telling clients, against my own best interests for closing loans, that they could not count on the property values not correcting. It was when one of my agents came to me saying that a bank had approved a parking valet for a million-dollar home that I realized I had a moral obligation to close down the company because I would not be part of putting people in future financial distress.

As a homebuyer, be careful of times like this. No matter who was at fault for the crash, homeowners should have seen those corrections coming. When the increases in land value had been steadily increasing by 8 to 10 percent each year and suddenly jumped to 20 percent, buyers should have stepped away from buying or refinancing their properties. Homeowners should not have taken vacations based on their unrealistic and impermanent equities. Please do not misunderstand me: I truly feel sad for those friends and clients I watched lose everything during those corrections. However, it is a reckless decision to overextend in a real estate market that is reaching outrageous increases.

If someone buys before a real estate slump like the one in 2006, they can lose money by selling too soon. But because of the birthrate, there will always be increasing long-term demand for property. Prices will recover and continue to grow at rates much higher than inflation.

A quick example of the constantly growing demand for real estate is the inexpensive farmland that investors buy up near growing cities to turn into new homes. The prices they offer to farmers are higher than the farmers can afford to refuse, forcing them to move their farms to cheaper, more distant land where they can buy much more farmland with the money. Land is in limited supply, and demand for it increases as each baby is born. Reliable estimates show that in the next ten years, there will be 10% more people in the world than there are today. This means that for every ten people in the world today, we will need to find room to fit one more on the land. Also consider that there will be 10% more people eating and buying products, and the farms, factories and stores will need to increase production accordingly. The only way this could change would be a catastrophic worldwide plague that increased the death rate over the birth rate, in which case we would have more to worry about than our investments.

It is extremely difficult for anyone to give exact figures for the value and profit of property ownership because there are so many ways to arrive at a number. I could simply pick the best method for my proof, but that would not be fair.

The US Census Bureau's statistics state that the "median home" in California has increased almost 100 times in value in the last 60 years (7.9% per year). This is misleading because what would be considered a "median home" today has changed. New upper-class homes are constantly being built in larger sizes, different shapes, and with expensive, top-grade building materials by well-paid union craftsmen. On the other side, inexpensive condos (which did not exist sixty years ago) are being churned out at relatively low cost. Sixty years ago, a large number of available homes were the two-bedroom post-WW2 square homes designed for returning soldiers. Comparing these very different types of houses runs into difficulties that make the "median price increase" of homes over the last sixty years a mathematically impossible figure to compute.

I could use the random example that my mother paid under $11,000 for her first home fifty years ago and recently saw the same aging home on the market for $750,000, showing an increase of 8.8% per year. Unlike with an investment such as comic books where only the lucky exceptions profit, in real estate this type of increase in property value is the norm. There are other factors that make the actual profit of the home higher than these figures: the home was purchased on leverage, gave tax benefits, and, most importantly, the owner lived in the house and therefore did not have to pay rent. The appreciation rate becomes much higher if you factor in all the advantages of owning property. Different time periods have returned different amounts of profit, but any span of over ten years will show at least an 8% appreciation in property value. In short, no one can give an exact figure for the increases in property value beyond the fact that they are higher than other investments and provide more benefits.

Anyone can own property. You don't have to open a brokerage or holding account, and you don't have to make a certain number of trades per year to keep active. People can steal your gold, your comics can turn to dust, your plates can break, but land lasts forever. With land, you can gain increased income from renting out the property or else save yourself from paying rent to someone else. We humans need to live someplace, and it costs money to live. Thus, your property is working for you, giving you profit beyond its increasing value.

Leverage
Leverage allows you to make a profit on other people's money. Let us say you put 20% down on a home valued fairly at $500,000, which you plan on renting out. Your investment was only $100,000, but you have $400,000 appreciating in value faster than the interest you are paying on the loan. You are also receiving the rent from a $500,000 home when you only have $100,000 invested. You are therefore getting five times the appreciation that a $100,000 investment would give you. If the value of the $500,000 home goes up 8% in a year to $540,000, you would have made $40,000 on a $100,000 investment, a return of 40%.

Here is a clearer way to look at leverage. Assume you spend $500,000 in cash for a house. In 5 years, at a realistic increase in value of 8%, the home will be worth $734,664. Now, assume instead that you buy five $500,000 homes, each with interest-only payments and down payments of $100,000 apiece. The cost would still be the same $500,000. However, you live in one, which saves you from renting, and rent the others out for enough to pay the mortgage and break about even each month. In five years, all the homes will be worth $734,664. You will now be controlling $3,673,320. Say you now sell everything. You had $500,000 invested and owe the bank $2,000,000, which means you made a profit of $1,173,320 in 5 years from $500,000 invested. This is 49% profit on your money, not including the free rent!

For those of you that understand ideas better looking at numbers, we will work out the above in more detail. I have picked easy, rounded numbers to keep this simple. In both of the scenarios below, the buyer will invest $500,000 of his own cash. All homes cost $500,000. The appreciation rate will be 8% per year. The loan is 6%, interest only, meaning that you pay the interest that accrues on the loan but do not put any money towards paying the loan off. Tenants in the area will pay $2,000 per month. We will see the potential difference between cash use and leverage.

Plan One: Invested 100% of $500,000 cash into ownership of one (1) rental home with no loan.

Plan Two: Invested 20% and a Loan To Value (LTV) of 80% into five (5) rental homes at $100,000 investment each. Total amount of controlled property is $2,500,000 (five homes X $500,000 each).

After one year:

	Plan One	Plan Two
New Value	$540,000	$2,700,000
Rental Income	$24,000	$120,000
Debt Paid at 6%	$0.	$120,000
Amount of Debt	$0.	$2,000,000
Value of Assets	$564,000	$2,700,000
Profit	$64,000	$200,000
Return on Investment	10.40%	40%

This becomes even more astronomical as the appreciation on the appreciation grows over the years.

After 10 years:

	Plan One	Plan Two
New Value	$1,079,463	$5,397,313
Rental Income	$240,000	$1,200,000
Debt Paid at 6%	$0.	$1,200,000
Amount of Debt	$0.	$2,000,000
Value of Assets	$1,319,463	$5,397,313
Profit	$819,463	$2,897,313
Return on Investment	115.89%	479.46%

Although I did not make a complete financial statement with costs such as repairs, vacancies, and property tax, I also did not increase the rents through the years, nor did I guess what your tax benefits would be. These things are too dependent on local factors for me to give an accurate figure. But you can see that leveraging at 20% down with a Loan To Value (LTV) of 80% will make over five times as much profit. Not everyone has $500,000 cash to invest, nor do homes in all places cost that much, but the same math can be used by adjusting the numbers to what you are dealing with. Using this example, we made many times our money in ten years. By taking whatever investment capital you have, you can see your estimated net profit over ten years by multiplying it by 25.73.

Tax Benefits
Taxes can be your friend when you don't pay them. Although I see freshly licensed real estate agents giving tax advice, I don't like to give it myself since everyone's situation is different. Furthermore, the law changes and loopholes can become very complicated. Different states may also have different benefits. In many places, if you make a good income on your normal job, you can show yearly "losses" on the property to defer payment on income to retain more of your yearly earnings.

At this point, you don't need to know about your tax benefits beyond the fact that you will have many of them. You will likely get tax credits for your home, you will likely be able to write off the interest you pay on any loans you use to leverage property, you will likely be able to defer paying any taxes on your profit even if you are exchanging profit (1031 exchange), you presently will be tax free on $250,000 of the profit on a principal residence held for over 2 years, and you will likely be able to keep a large amount of your profit when you decide to sell. The more money you keep working for you before paying your taxes, the more profit you can make on that money.

Control
The most important benefit of property investment may be that you are the one controlling your destiny. Unlike your stocks where you don't have many voting rights in the operation of the company, with your own property you make the decisions. You pick the property, you decide how much you are willing to pay, you decide how much to repair the property, you decide whether to rent it out, to whom, and for how much, and you decide when to sell it.

None of the other types of investments can compete with the profit you can make by leveraging your money into real estate. With real estate, you can buy with little or nothing down, you can buy at below the going value, and you can pick the type and location of your property to

14

guarantee the highest appreciation. You will know how to do all these things by the time you finish this book.

2.   What Is Real Estate?

Even real estate professionals get confused by some of the terms used when dealing with property. In law school, my fellow students had more difficulty with the concepts of property than any other area of law. This is because the practices and terminology of land ownership go back to the time of William the Conqueror. In order to understand how real property *works,* it is most helpful to know how it *came about*. I have found the best way to teach how real property works (even to attorneys) is to look at the question: "What would William do?" I will give some fun history (with a little writer's embellishment) to get everyone to the same starting point.

William created the leasing of land, and after his death his son Henry the First dealt with the sale of the land. Let's just make it easy and give William the full credit during our story. We will be using farms and blacksmith shops as examples, but the same ideas work today with homes and commercial buildings.

William the Conqueror
In the year 1066, William the Conqueror captured the land now known as England. He was a great warrior. He took all the land he could see and united England under one rule: his own! But once the fighting was done, it took him a while to learn how to manage his land. Now that William owned all that land, he could charge people for living and working on it. He now had the right to decide whom to put on each piece of land and how to take a percentage of the profits to operate his kingdom. There were, by most estimates, over a million people living under William's rule, and the management of those people was taking an army of accountants with quill pens. The simplest answer seemed to be to hire a governor to oversee local teams of accountants in each town and tax each person based on income. But not only would it be hard to know how much each person made in order to figure the tax, but the governors could run off with the money or do their jobs badly, and the people were less motivated to work hard when the tax man took their profits. William wanted the best use of the land, and this type of management did not

16

motivate people to use the land for the highest and best purposes.

William also had problems with how to receive taxes from people that lived hundreds of miles away in the days before the fax machine or cell phone. He figured out that it would be easier to have negotiators set fair payments to be due once per a period of time than to have accountants frisking people's pockets each week to see how much they had made.

Instead of trying to control all the land himself or trying to find someone honest in each area to govern it for him, William found it was easier to find people who would manage the land for him for a fixed amount and allow them to keep the rest of their profits. You can think of this as similar to the system franchises such as McDonald's use. The fast food chain allows someone else to own the local store, and that person pays a fixed sum to the main company. The owner works hard because he keeps the profit he makes, making the business more likely to succeed. The company makes its prearranged amount of money and does not have to go through the trouble of micromanaging each location. Basing his choices on whom he trusted and to whom he owed moral debts, William found several ways of handing over control while still receiving a fixed profit from the use of his land.

Before we can let William give away any rights, we first need to look at what ownership William had to give. William had the rights to his property from the center of the earth all the way to the heavens. No one could tell William what to do with his land because he owned it outright with no debt. No one could take it from him by any method short of warfare. He had a **"Fee Simple Absolute."** In spite of the debts, eminent domain, easements, leases, etc. that we have on property today, we still use that term. If a person today is on title as the owner of the land, and there is no restriction that interferes with his rights to keep the land, we call it a Fee Simple.

We must understand what real property is before we can own it or trade it. There are three types of "property" that may be owned: Intellectual Property, Personal Property, and Real Property. **Intellectual Property** is the rights to an idea, like Walt Disney's rights to Mickey Mouse. **Personal Property** is anything that may be moved. **Real Property** is anything attached to the land and not (easily) movable. For example, William can hold a nail in his hand, and this is Personal Property because it can be moved. If he hammers it into the wall, it becomes unmovable

17

(without using force) and is now Real Property. If he now hangs a picture, which is Personal Property, on that nail, he can still lift off it easily, and so it remains Personal Property. When trading real estate, make sure it is clear in the contract what is personal property, or there may be arguments when the seller takes the dishwasher or doorknobs away with him.

Transferring property rights
There are many rights to land, and they can be transferred separately. A person can have rights to mineral deposits or water on the property, rights to cross the land, or rights to use the land. Even time on the land can be traded, as with a rental agreement or timeshare. You must understand that land can be cut up not only by borders but also in ownership, time, and use.

With the ownership of land, there comes what is termed the **Bundle of Rights**. Although many books have been written on just this topic, all you need to know is a quick overview. The rights of ownership include the right to occupancy and use, the right to exclude others, the right to sell in whole or in part, the right to bequeath (decide who will inherit it from you), the right to transfer for specified periods of time, and the right to the benefits from the leasing or use of the property. Any of those rights can be sold without selling the whole property, and a person can sell most of the rights, keeping only a few for himself. An example of this would be the seller keeping the right to use the pond to fish or keeping the mineral rights to drill for oil even after selling the other rights to the property. Because of all the individual rights to the land, there are a lot of different ways to sell the property to make a profit. When buying a home in today's world, we rarely receive the full "bundle of rights," because some past developer will usually have sold the mineral rights or created utilities easements.

The easiest way for William to make sure he receives a profit from his land would be to **sell** outright all his rights to the property to another. This way, William has all his money up front, and the problem of how to manage the property is in the hands of the new landowner who now has the fee simple.

If a buyer does not have the money to purchase at the time of the sale, the buyer and William may agree to a **Land Contract**. Here, William keeps the fee simple to the land but hands over the right to use it to the other person. This person can profit from the land, but must pay William a fixed amount of money each year until he has paid the full price for the land. Imagine a farmer buying land gradually by giving most of his profits to the landowner until he has paid enough to keep the land in fee simple. This can benefit both sides: William has his yearly profit from the land but does not have to manage it. The farmer has full control of the land and is using the proceeds of his work on it to buy it. Eventually, the farmer will pay off William for the Fee Simple and be able to keep all his profits. If the farmer mismanages the land and can't make the payments, William will take the land back to sell it to someone else who can manage it better.

A **lease** is a transfer of the right to occupy and use the land for a period of time. William transfers the rights to use some land to a tenant who pays a fee each year to use it. William has a guaranteed amount of income from the land and the tenant, particularly in the case of leased farmland, may make a profit from the land for a fixed sum. William never gives up his ownership. William is termed the lessor and the person who leases the land is the lessee. When the term of the lease ends, the tenant can renew the lease for a new term or William can find a new tenant to lease the use of the land to.

The **"ee" and "or"** used in legal talk confuses people, but once explained, it is easy to understand. The end of the word indicates the position of each person in a contract. The "or" is the person doing an action, and the "ee" is the person the action is being done to. A person leasing their land is the lessor; a person agreeing to the lease contract is the lessee. A person that trusts a person is a trustor; the person that is trusted is the trustee. A person that assigns his rights is the assignor; the person taking the rights is the assignee. These terms apply to their actions in a particular contract. People may have different contracts and have different designations in each one. A lessee of one contract could sublease the property and in that sublease contract would be the sublessor. To keep this from being confusing, think only of the contract being discussed and the person's actions in that contract. <u>In every agreement, there is a "Do-or" and a "Do-ee."</u>

A lease may sound a lot like a land contract, but there are some major differences. The most important is that with a lease, William never intends to hand over more than the right to occupy the property for a period of time. The cost the tenant pays will be a lot less than in a land contract because nothing is going to the sales price. Remember, a farmer who enters into a land contract puts his profits towards owning the land outright, while a farmer who leases keeps the profit he makes on the farm, minus the rent he pays to William.

A **sublease** occurs when a person (the lessee) that leases land from William (the lessor) allows a different person use some part of that land for a fee. The lessee is still a "lessee" in the contract to William but becomes a sublessor in the contract with the sublessee. Note that not all the original rights of the lessee have to be given to the new person. The lessee may have had a 5-year lease and only subleased the first 3 years to the new sublessee, or may have rented a 2-bedroom house and subleased only 1 room to a roommate. The lessee who rents from William keeps some rights that he does not sublease.

This is different from an **Assignment**. In an assignment, the new person steps in and takes all of the lessee's rights, time and duties. Nothing is left in the hands of the original lessee except legal responsibility if the new person does not perform on the contract with William.

A **Novation** is when the lessee has been replaced by a new person with the approval of the lessor. The original lessee is no longer on the contract and has no legal responsibilities for the behavior of the new tenant.

A **Lease option** is when the tenant pays a little extra over the cost of a normal lease each month to make William hold the sales price of the farm constant for the tenant, in case the tenant chooses to buy. Let's say the value of the farm is $100,000 today, and that the fair lease price is $1,000 a month. The tenant pays $1,200 a month and, at any time during the lease, can buy the farm for the $100,000 fixed amount. The tenant has bet that the land may be worth a lot more in the future and he will have the money then to buy the farm at only today's value. William is betting the tenant will not be able to buy the property in five years and that William will have made an extra $200 a month from rent. Even if the tenant can come up with the money, William still receives the $100,000 the property was worth when the contract started and an extra $12,000 beyond the normal rent over the five years.

This may sound almost like a Land Contract. The difference is that in a land contract, the tenant is purchasing the property over time, and there is a preset date at which the property will be handed over to the new owner. In a Lease Option, the tenant was only paying a little more each month to keep the right to buy the property, and none of those payments went to the sales price.

An easement is the right to use the land of another. Let us say that William is willing to lease or sell land for the grazing of cattle, but that land blocks the fastest way for William's wagons to get to the shipping docks. William can retain the right to travel across that land, either on a particular road or anywhere he wants to travel, depending on the contract. Since property rights can be sold separately, someone can sell just an easement to cross his land. Today, almost every property has some easements on it so the power, sewage, cable, and phone lines can get to your home and the homes around you.

Ways to Hold Property
It can be very important how the ownership of a property is recorded. Property can be recorded under an individual's name, several people's names, or different forms of corporations. Although in some cases one person may have a fee simple with the full bundle of rights, in other cases several people can have ownership rights to the same land, one with the right for the minerals, one with the right of easement, one with the right to occupy, and so on. No matter what rights you have, you still need to "record" those rights with the county for protection. Different states may have different names for ownership and ways to handle this. There can be far-ranging implications for ownership decisions, depending on the eventual sale of the property, death of an owner, taxation, and state laws. Real estate agents may be exceeding their expertise in giving advice on this. It is best to get the advice of a financial planning attorney, but few buyers are willing to pay for that information.

To keep this from becoming too complicated for our purposes, we will assume all the below people have a fee simple. These are the standard rules:

John Doe as _____, Sole Ownership
This is stating that John Doe is the one and only owner of the property in fee simple and has full rights to do with the property as he wishes. The difference will be in the words that follow his name. John Doe is male in our example, but the terms may apply to a woman in the same way.

John Doe as a **single man**: this gives notice to the world that John has never been married, and no ex-spouse may jump in to claim that part of her money was used to buy the property.

John Doe as a **married man**: this gives notice that John has a wife, and, if he lacks some documents stating otherwise, she may claim some ownership in the property, especially if they are in a state that follows the community property laws.

John Doe as an **unmarried man**: this gives notice that John *does* have an ex-wife who may claim her money was used to buy the property.

John Doe and Suzy Doe, community property
Here we know that a married couple has the rights to the property, and if one should die, his or her last testament or the state laws may affect the ownership. Only some states and U.S. territories recognize community property, and their laws may differ in how the property is treated. Both people need to approve the sale and encumbering (leasing and borrowing).

John Doe and Curly Smith, as Tenants in Common
Do not confuse this with leasing or renting because of the word "tenant"; this is a form of ownership. In this case, John and Curly each own the rights to an undivided percentage of the property. Either one can freely sell or borrow against his own share only. Depending on the contract, these percentages do not have to be equal, and there can be many co-owners of the property if all are listed on the title. Think of this as a partnership. Let us say there is an apartment building where John owns 50%, Curly owns 25%, and Ann owns 25%, and they are all tenants in common. Maybe none of them actually lives in the building, but they share in the profits from the rent proportionally to their percentages of the ownership. A lender that was only in contract with Curly and who then foreclosed would only get Curly's 25%. Banks are therefore only willing to contract loans that involve all the owners.

John Doe and Curly Smith, Joint Tenants with right of survivorship
The tricky part of this form of ownership is that all the owners must have equal shares and rights, acquired at the same time with the same paperwork. When one of the people dies, the other owners automatically take the dead person's shares in the property. This situation will happen when a person's last testament says "To my children as joint tenants."

This ensures that the property will stay in the family for as long as there is at least one surviving child. Domestic partners often use this where they cannot take advantage of the marital laws of their state. Often an elderly parent will add an adult child to avoid probate.

Historically, once in a joint tenancy, one owner could not sell without all parties selling, but this created a number of problems. Nowadays, the courts promote the free exchange of property, and a joint tenant may sell his rights, forcing the other owners into a tenancy in common with the person who buys the sold share. For example, two sisters buy some land this way and each counts on owning it outright if she lives the longest. However, right before one dies, she transfers her share to a boyfriend, and on her death, the living sister and the dead sister's boyfriend are equal 50% owners. This problem does not happen often, but people entering into a joint tenancy should know and trust their co-owners.

Future Interests:
The following terms are complicated and rarely used in modern times. Few professionals ever have to deal with them. However, this book would be far from complete without a quick overview, in case you ever come across them. Unless you are a real estate professional or they apply to something you are dealing with, feel free to skip ahead to the beginning of the next chapter.

Future interests originated from William's desire to control how people used his property. In the following examples, the ostensible owners of the properties do not hold the fee simples because some restriction hangs over the property that can or will cause it to transfer into the hands of another person.

Life Estate
A person has the right to occupy the land during the life of a designated person. When the designated person dies, the property transfers to someone else. An example would be if William gave the use of a blacksmith shop to Jim as long as Jim was alive, then William would get the land back. Nowadays, you will see this when a last testament states, "I give a life estate to my wife as long as she lives, then to my son." The wife can use the land only as long as she lives, and when she dies, the son gets a fee simple to the land. The wife can sell the use of the land to Mary, but not the ownership. When the wife dies, Mary has nothing, and the son takes everything. The life used to measure how long the

designated person may use the home can be anyone's life. The deed could say, "To my wife as long as her sister lives, then to my son." The important thing to understand is that the wife may only use the property until the mentioned person dies, then the property goes to someone else.

Right of Reversion

The person who owns the property deeds the property to someone "for as long as," "while," or "during" some occurrence. Imagine that William deeds the property, but fears that an opposing army will mass on the land. William makes the provision that if such a thing happens, he instantly gets his land back. Or maybe William only wants to have the land used for a farm or a church. If the new owner changes the use, it becomes William's land again, whether or not William still wants it. In modern times, people sometimes donate property "as long as" it is used for charity. This way, if the charity abuses the rights of the free gift and decides to sell it to a business many years later, the gift giver gets the property back. If the gift giver is no longer alive, whoever received the rights from the gift giver's last testament will get the property. Almost any restriction can be put on property this way, but it is subject to rules of public policy. For instance, this cannot be used for racial discrimination.

Right of Entry

This is very similar to right of reversion above, except that under right of entry, violation of the clause allows the original owner to decide whether he will step in and take the property back. The wording can sound similar, but the difference is the right of decision. Phrases that signal that right of entry is in effect are "on condition," "if used for," or "provided that." Imagine that William deeds a granary to someone "provided that" the grain made will never be used for beer and beer will never be drunk on the land. Twenty years later, the granary accidentally sells some grain to a brewery, and an employee is caught drinking beer in the granary. William now has a choice of whether he will take the property back based on the violation or decide that he really does not care to own it.

Condition Precedent

Here, William can force a person to take an action before that person can acquire the property. If the person fails to meet the requirement, he forfeits his rights to ownership. William could say that he will give the castle to his son if the son marries within 5 years. The son will have a deed in his hands but cannot have or use the property until he marries. If the son does not marry within those 5 years, the deed becomes useless and William regains his fee simple to the castle. In modern times, a parent could put in a will, "to my son, provided he finishes college."

Remainders: Executory or Reversion

All of the above forms of ownerships raise the question: *Who gets the property after the current state of ownership ends?* Who, for instance, gets the castle if William's son does not marry? Whatever rights are left over are called "remainders." If what is left could go back to the original owner (William) or his heirs, there is a "possibility of reverter." If the original owner (William) states that the property will go to a third person, then there is an "executory interest." In the example where William gave the property to his wife for her lifetime and then to his son, the son has an executory interest.

The rules against perpetuities

These rules are restrictions on what can be done, not ways of transferring property. They can be extremely complex, and if you ever come across them, don't walk, *run* to an expert. The idea behind these rules is that land should not be set aside for some great, great, great grandchild, but should always be moving and be used for the "highest and best use." However, there are some deeds where the rights of ownership may not vest (meaning no one has the rights to them) for years. The length of time in which a property does not vest cannot exceed the life of a person (any person) plus 21 years. An example of a violation of the rule would be "to my wife for life, then to all of our grandchildren that reach 30 years of age." If the wife dies while none of William's children have children themselves yet (or any children they do have are under 9 years old), there will be no grandchildren over 30 within 21 years. Full libraries of books have been written trying to figure out the more complicated instances of this, and the laws may be different in different states. But don't worry too much: you will probably never see this, and if it ever does come up, the title company will spot it for you.

All the above terms can be mixed and matched to create very complicated situations: "To my wife for life, then to my son if he is married at that time, if not, to the children of my daughter who are 20 years old at the time as joint tenants with right of survivorship, and if there be no such person, then to the heirs of my first wife as tenants in common as long as they never serve alcohol on the property, reserving a right of remainder in my heirs." Fortunately, cases of this are very rare.

3. Who are all the players?

Real estate has contracts, and contracts involve the law. There are many different terms to describe people, depending on what actions they are performing at a given time. A person may have several different descriptors at the same time. Let's go through the list of people you will deal with, what they are called, and what their duties are.

Principals are the buyers and sellers of the property. They either have or will be acquiring some interest in the property. All the other people involved in the transaction will be assisting the principals in properly completing their contract for the exchange of the property.

In order to represent one of the principals in a real estate transaction, a person must be licensed as a **broker** in the state where the property exists by having complied with the state's educational requirements and passed a test. The broker has the ultimate legal and monetary responsibility for the actions his office performs. The broker usually owns the office, reviews ongoing sales, and runs the business. The broker cannot be in all places at all times, so he has "agents" representing him and doing the legwork. The agent can spend quality time helping the principals so that the busy broker's time is only taken up if a question arises that is beyond the agent's knowledge.

Agents have more relaxed educational requirements and less complicated tests to pass for their licensing. An agent may not represent a principal without being connected to a broker who oversees the agent's actions. This is often referred to as "hanging on the broker's wall," indicating that the agent's license is supposedly framed in the office of the broker. Some agents like to refer to themselves as "brokers." This common activity is of questionable legality, and they do it to make themselves sound more qualified than they are. Ask anyone claiming to be a "broker" whether he is really a "broker" or an "agent." Dealing with an agent is by no means a bad thing; it is often better than dealing with a broker because an agent will actually have time for you. While there are many agents who only work in real estate as a side job and whose talents are limited to showing homes, others are well-seasoned, top professionals who keep up with the current laws. Some agents are more experienced than some brokers, but if you need complex advice, it is wisest not to take it from an agent unless you know his qualifications.

Agents are subcontractors for the broker rather than employees. The brokers usually do not pay their subcontractors payroll, do not supply insurance, and do not take taxes out of the commissions their agents receive.

Being subcontractors allows the agents a lot of leeway in their schedules and methods of operation. Agents work when and where they want and make their money on commission. The agent will have made a contract with the broker on what percentage of the commission the agent will receive, and that amount depends on the experience and quality of the agent. A new agent who requires the broker's close supervision may only keep 50% of the commissions he makes, with the broker keeping the rest to pay for the time spent on the agent's training. A more experienced agent will keep more. Some brokers even offer 100% commission to the experienced agent, if the agent pays a monthly fee. An agent may not legally receive any direct payment from anyone he is assisting in a duty requiring a license. The broker receives all funds to disburse.

The agents and brokers have different titles depending on whom they represent. This can get confusing. The agent working for the seller is called either the **seller's agent** or the **listing agent** because he took the original listing on the property from the seller. The agent that brings the buyer is called the **buyer's agent**. Once a contract has been signed, the buyer's agent becomes the **selling agent**, because he actually sold the property. Don't confuse this with the "seller's agent," who represents the seller!

Sometimes the agent that listed the property also brings the buyer and sells the property. This "double agency" can get a little sticky because it usually means the agent's primary loyalty and legal responsibility remain with the seller. In these cases, the buyer may not be properly represented in negotiations. Many principals like having only one agent involved because there is no possibility of dispute between the agents. However, having the seller's agent advising the buyer on how much the property is worth creates a conflict of interest.

Real estate is complicated and varied, and even brokers are not expected to know all the laws and types of transactions. Although agents do their best to be informed, do not assume their knowledge is equal to that of a broker. I have seen many agents make statements that were incorrect or against their fiduciary duty (legal obligation to act in a client's best interests) to the principals. On one occasion, an agent told me he was allowed to park in the red (no parking) zone because he was an "agent." Think of the relationship between the agent and the broker as similar to that between a nurse and a doctor. In theory, a nurse could have so much practical experience and years of additional schooling that his knowledge surpasses that of the doctor. But unless I am sure of the particular nurse, I feel more comfortable knowing nurses are under the watchful eyes of doctors.

Realtors ® belong to a national organization for brokers and agents. A broker does not need to be a Realtor to represent principals. It may be easiest to think of this organization as a club. People join, pay fees, and receive benefits. Most local communities have their own group of Realtors, called a Board. The organization offers many services to the brokers and agents, including selling blank contracts, offering classes, offering insurance, selling signs, etc. Most importantly, they offer access to the **Multiple Listing Service (MLS).** This is a password-protected website on which brokers list the homes they are under contract to sell in hopes that a different broker has a buyer who may be interested. Brokers usually state they will "cooperate" (pay) a percentage of their commission to anyone licensed who brings a buyer for the listed property.

The antitrust laws forbid a unified set rate for the commission a seller will pay or how much cooperation (pay) will be given to the agent who brings a buyer. Unfortunately, human nature is such that the buyer's agent will often first show a buyer the properties that offer the agent the highest commissions, regardless of the needs of the buyer. The MLS states how much cooperation will be given to the buyer's agent, and that agent can fail to show the buyer homes for which the seller's agent does not offer enough cooperation.

After the seller and buyer have formed a contract, experts in the transfer of property step in to help complete the deal. These people include escrow officers, title agents, mortgage brokers, appraisers, and inspectors.

The **escrow office** is a neutral third party that assists the principals in the exchange. It assigns each transaction an **escrow officer** whose job is to make sure the money and property are exchanged at the exact same time. This is important because a buyer does not want to hand over cash to the seller and then cross his fingers and hope the seller really hands over the house. Likewise, the bank does not want to give you a check for a loan and hope you really use it to buy a house. In order to make sure that everything occurs as the contract dictates, the escrow office has a computer program that lists all the paperwork and tasks that must first be performed. After all paperwork is signed and the funds are deposited in the escrow account, the escrow agent will distribute the property, commissions, and funds appropriately.

Title Companies sell a one-time insurance policy to verify that the seller has the right to sell the property. These companies compete for your agent's business and generally are extremely helpful in supplying information in the hopes of attracting agents. If at any time in the future someone pops up and claims they own your property, the title company's attorneys will protect your rights to the property. If their lawyers lose, they will make you financially whole from any losses you received. Before records were as well kept as they are today, this was a very important service. Nowadays, there are rarely ambiguities about who has the right to sell a property. The cost for this service is very low, and no lender would loan on a property without such a policy.

The **Financial Institution (FI)**, sometimes called the **Investor, Bank** or **Lender,** is the company that actually lends the money to the homebuyer. Some FIs deal directly with the buyers, and others only deal through mortgage brokers. Most FIs resell the bulk of the mortgage debts they own to bigger FIs or to government-backed FIs like Fannie Mae or Freddie Mac.

In rare instances, there will be a **private lender** making what is sometimes called a **hard money loan**. These lenders are usually businesses not normally in the lending business, but can also be individuals. Private lenders loan the funds when the buyer does not qualify under the FI's requirements. The private lender will be more lenient concerning the buyer's credit scores or income, but will almost always change much higher fees and interest because of the greater risk.

A **mortgage broker,** also known as a **loan broker,** operates similarly to the real estate broker, including having subcontracted agents, but specializes in helping the buyer find loans. The loan broker works exclusively for the buyer. The real estate agents cannot demand that the buyer use a particular loan broker, though many real estate brokers have an in-house loan broker they recommend.

Since most FIs also loan money directly to the homebuyer, you may ask why you should use a loan broker at all. The answer is that if you have good credit and can qualify, you are usually better off dealing directly with the FI (often a bank) for terms and rates, which they will state upfront. A buyer with less than optimal credit, however, can walk into many banks and be turned down by all of them, but the broker will already have figured out which FIs will accept the buyer based on the different FI programs, and will prepare the paperwork. You will sometimes do better through a loan broker even if you are the optimal buyer because those brokers pass the loans on to the FIs at wholesale (less than advertised to the public) rates. The loan broker may know where you can get a better rate or which FIs will accept you, and could theoretically get you a better deal. Remember, however, that the loan broker will take some cut for this profit, that not all loan brokers will pass the savings on to you, and that some will add many extra fees.

Appraisers value the property for the buyer. There are two reasons for an appraiser. The first is that the buyer wants to make sure he is not getting a bad price on the property, and the second is that the FI wants to make sure it is not loaning based on more than the property is worth for purposes of the security of repayment.

Inspectors. Whether they are looking for termites, ground movement, another specialized concern, or performing basic inspections, home inspectors verify that the buyer knows exactly what he is buying. Most buyers are not experts in all areas, so the inspectors supply reliable information to the buyer concerning the condition of the property. Even having a contractor's license myself, I still use inspectors because I want a neutral person making the report. Always pick your own inspectors or have one referred to you by your agent. Don't accept a recommendation from the seller, even if he claims the inspector is "neutral."

4.   A Transaction: What Is Really Going On?

Great! Now that we are both using the same terms, we can discuss what is happening behind the scenes in real estate transactions. You may be saying to yourself, "Why would I care?" But the more you know, the easier it is to make things happen the way you want and the better you can act to protect your money. After all, this is about your money. You want to make the best profit with the least amount of work and costs. No matter what titles and experience the people working for you may claim, it is wisest not to simply assume they are acting in your best interest. Don't get me wrong: most people do their jobs and want to help you. But it is *your* money. You should know where it is going.

If you have never bought a home or did not know what was going on behind the scenes when you did, this is a great walkthrough. Even many agents do not know what is happening in the different offices involved in completing the deal. All the training in the world cannot equal first-hand experience, but with this walkthrough you'll be able to see this situation play out as if you had experienced it. The next time you are involved in buying property, you'll be able to say to yourself at any stage in the process, "All right, I know what's happening. I've seen this before."

We will go through all the events of a fairly standard transaction together. Things will go wrong in our example; I would be hard-pressed to recall a transaction where everything went perfectly smoothly. While some problems do arise from people misrepresenting their abilities, even the most experienced people make mistakes. Even personalities can destroy a deal. I once had a seller overhear the buyer saying what color he was going to repaint a room, and despite my best efforts to explain to the seller that the house would belong to the buyer and he could do what he liked with it, the seller threw the buyer out of the house.

Problems arise that the principals hear nothing about, sometimes leading to delays nobody will explain to them. Principals can find themselves

31

trapped and overwhelmed, wondering what happened and whether they could have protected themselves from it. Believe me, the example that follows is not uncommon, and much worse things have happened.

I will describe what the principals see in normal typeface. *I will use bold/italic type for the events behind closed doors.*

The Sally and Brad Deal:

Sally (the homeowner) owns a Single Family Residence (SFR) and decides on the first of January to sell the property and move to a nearby town for a better job. Sally knows that three months ago the house across the street sold for $400,000. She assumes her home will make the same amount of money or more. Sally owes her bank (the FI) $300,000 on the home loan. Sally calculates she will make $100,000 profit to use as a down payment to buy her new home.

Sally doesn't know what agent to use, so she looks through the drawer of accumulated calendars and notepads advertising real estate sales agents' names that she's received in the mail over the years.

Most large real estate offices separate the territory of where their agents may advertise so that their agents don't compete directly within their own office. This is called a **farm.** *In hopes of getting their business, the title insurance companies supply the agents with lists of owner's names from the county recorder's office. The agents use that list to send out letters and other advertising material to all the people on their farm.*

Unsure of whom to call, Sally calls a local, well-known real estate office and talks to Abe, the agent who answers the phone.

Large offices let different agents have "floor time," where the agent gets the exclusive right to market to anyone that calls the office during his shift. The better and more experienced agents tend to be too busy to sit floor time: therefore Abe is probably inexperienced. Had Sally checked around for an agent with many homes listed for sale in her area, she would likely have found someone both active and experienced.

Sally and Abe make an appointment for Abe to review the home. Abe goes on the **Multiple Listing Service (MLS)** and, using Sally's address, creates a **Comparative Market Analysis (CMA)** to use as a selling method for Sally.

The CMA is a very rough appraisal of the home's value based on local sale information. There is an art to creating a relatively accurate CMA. An experienced agent, which Abe is not, knows that there's a big difference in the prices of homes listed and homes sold—homes listed may overstate the value, but if Abe only bases his appraisal on sold homes, his CMA may not reflect the value growth in the community. He needs to consider carefully how long different homes have been on the market and for what prices to get an idea of what people are really willing to pay. Slight differences in the radius he enters into the search field may matter a great deal or not at all, depending on the better and worse neighborhoods in the area. Different agents can come up with different CMA values for the same home.

Abe shows up at Sally's house at the appointed time in his only suit and an expensive rental car.

I have never personally understood why ostentatious displays of wealth give people more faith in an agent, but I can't deny that it works. I have shown up in different clothes and found the more glittery gold I wear, the better my return on selling.

Abe's impressive business card states in gold leaf that he is in the "Millionaire's Club."

This probably means Abe sold one million dollars worth of property in one year. Many years ago, when homes in good neighborhoods cost under $50,000, this may have meant closing 20 large homes in one year—a noteworthy accomplishment. But in my part of the world, a nice home costs over one million, and one big sale in a year would put me in the club.

Abe tells Sally that all agents charge 6% commission to sell a home.

It is against the law to price fix the commission to sell real property— therefore Abe's claim that "all agents" do this is false. However, I happen to agree that in the competitive world of brokers, depending on demand in the area, 6% is usually about fair. By negotiating too low a *commission, the seller may discourage the agent from doing the job with all diligence. Assume the average agent lists and sells five $500,000 homes a year in his area, which would be sales of $2,500,000. Six percent is $150,000, and half of that goes to the buyer's agents. The broker's office takes about 30%, leaving the agent with $52,500, minus advertising and other costs. Most areas do not average $500,000 homes, and most agents do not sell five houses a year. In order to qualify for a loan on a home in the area he lives in, an agent would have to sell about eight homes a year.*

Abe tells Sally he will do a lot of work to market and sell her home.

Unless Abe states in the listing agreement or some other signed document how he will market the property (such as how many open houses, etc.), Abe is not required to spend money or time to do anything. He has a fiduciary duty (responsibility) to the seller, but the law is unclear about what that entails. Some agents work hard to sell their listed houses, but others play a game of numbers: if they have enough listings, some will sell even with no effort on the agent's part.

Abe determines the home is worth $440,000. The other people Sally talked to gave estimates of $350,000, $375,000, $400,000, and $425,000. Since Abe says he will get her more for her property, she makes a listing with Abe.

Abe may really have thought the house was worth that much money, but sometimes less scrupulous agents will overprice a home to give false hope to the seller and keep the sale out of the hands of the more reasonable agents. After a few months without interested buyers, the agent talks the seller into a lower price. Other agents deliberately undervalue homes to guarantee quick sales and their own commissions.

They sign a **listing contract** saying that Abe's broker has the right to sell the property for the next 6 months.

Since Abe is really a subcontractor working exclusively for his broker, the listing contract Sally signed with Abe is really an agreement with the broker.

Almost everything on the contract is negotiable. Depending on how active the buyers are in the area, Sally could have given less time to Abe in the contract to find a buyer.

Abe puts the listing on the MLS so that all the agents in town can see it. Abe does some calculations, thinks about how empty his pockets are, and figures out that he would make more money if he only shares 2% out of his own 6% with any agent who brings a buyer.

This is a major mistake. Other agents may offer 3% commission splits or more, and by only offering 2%, Abe makes buyer's agents unwilling to show the property. Sally's home will not get full exposure, and Sally has no way of knowing Abe is doing this. Sally could, however, have put in the original listing contract how much Abe must pay in cooperation to other agents.

Abe spends his own money to make up signs and pamphlets. He then sets up a broker's open house on a weekday. Herds of agents pile through the home and leave their business cards. Sally is impressed with Abe's efforts and his connections with other agents.

Most "brokers' open houses" on weekdays (as opposed to the ones on weekends intended for the general public) are purely social events for agents, with attendance based on who has the better free food. Sure, there may be a few agents previewing homes for the needs of their potential buyers, but agents have an unspoken agreement to attend each other's broker's opens to make them look good to the new client. Nonetheless, these functions are important. If your agent is not putting out the $50 for food or getting some of the hopeful outside services (title, escrow, loan, inspectors) to do it for him, he is not properly promoting your property.

Three months have passed. Sally has been keeping her home spotless and she needs to move soon, but few buyers have come by, and none has been interested.

Two reasons: first, it is winter, and Abe did not explain to Sally that most people like to buy homes in the summer months, not only because of the weather but so their kids will not have to transfer schools in the middle of the year. Second, Abe promised a price far over the value of the home.

Abe and Sally agree to reduce the asking price to $410,000, and Abe raises his offer to other agents to 2.5% for finding a buyer. Abe then makes a sign that says "Reduced $30,000!" and puts it in front of the house.

Strangely, buyers get excited that they are getting a good deal when the price is "reduced." All it is really saying is that no buyer wanted the house for the first asking price.

An agent named Andy brings by a buyer named Brad. Andy uses his common key to open the house and shows Brad the home. Brad loves the home and thinks to himself that he wants to make an offer. Although Andy had been spending every day for weeks showing Brad homes, Brad has a sister-in-law named Ann out of town who has an agent's license. Brad lies to Andy and tells him he changed his mind about buying a home. Brad calls Ann, excited that he found the perfect home and asks her to write up an offer for him.

The agent that shows the home to the client is his legal agent. Unscrupulous buyers take up the time, trouble, and expenses of an agent only to abandon the agent at the last minute and get a relative to write the offer. This is a civil matter, and even if Andy suspects, he probably cannot prove that Brad and Ann conspired to deceive him. Andy did the work, spent gas money, took Brad to lunch every day, and wasted his own valuable time, but he is now out of the deal.

Ann, with the help of her broker Bob, checks over the listing and makes a **purchase offer** for Brad to sign. Bob, the experienced broker, notices that the MLS lists the sale of the home as contingent on "Seller to find home of choice." Bob writes on the offer that this clause will have no effect.

Sellers like to say they have the right to find a new home before buyers takes their old homes, but this ties up the contract and leaves the buyer with nothing if the seller does not find a home. Sometimes it is written that the seller's other deal must close, and this can take months. Meanwhile, the buyer cannot make an offer on a different house because he has made a contractual deal to buy the first house if he can.

Bob then does his own CMA to help Ann advise Brad on how much to offer, and suggests $390,000. Despite the good advice, Brad wants to get a great deal and only offers $350,000 for the house. They write up and sign a purchase offer contract and deliver it to Abe.

Getting a great price is something all buyers want, but if the initial offer is too ridiculously low, it becomes an insult to the seller. An insulted seller may cut off future negotiations, even if the buyer later offers an acceptable price. Before making a "low ball" offer, research the home and seller. Sometimes there are situations that could cause a low offer to be agreeable.

Abe looks at it the low offer and tells Ann it is too low and he will not show it to Sally.

This is illegal: all offers must be communicated to the seller. Abe is an agent and cannot make the decision to reject an offer.

Abe decides to tell Sally about the low offer just to show her that his marketing campaign is working. Sally is excited and says she would like to counter the offer at $405,000. They make a **counter offer** and Abe takes it to Ann. Ann and Abe talk bluntly about how they can make this deal work so they both get paid. Together they admit that their clients have told them <u>confidentially</u> that they would be willing to agree at $400,000. Ann advises Brad to make a counter offer to the counter offer at $400,000 because someone else is starting to bid on the property.

This is a common practice, and very wrong. It is Ann and Abe's job to negotiate for the principals. By telling each other their clients' confidential upper and lower bounds, they have removed the principals' ability to negotiate. Also, they are unethically pretending a competition where there is none. The agents are prioritizing their own commissions over their duty to look out for their clients. Principals have no reason to tell their agents how much they will move to on a deal and should keep that information to themselves.

Abe and Ann draw up a contract they both know their principals will sign. They disagree on what services (title company, escrow office, termite inspector) to use, but eventually decide that each will let their own friends do some of the services, and they finish the contract.

Services are not allowed to pay the agents for referring them, but agents can feel indebted to a service because of small gifts or personal relationships. I have actually seen agents willing to destroy an agreement because their friends' services were not being used.

Before handing the agreement to Sally, Abe requests that Brad get a "lender's pre-qualification" so that he can tell Sally it is likely Brad really can afford to buy the house.

*A **lender's pre-qualification** is useless because it does not claim the client can get a loan. All it means is that the lender knows of the buyer and, based on a quick phone call, thinks the buyer may be able to get a loan. Nothing has been verified. A lender will often hand over a pre-qualification even if they believe it would be hard for the buyer to qualify, because having helped the buyer increases the likelihood that the buyer will use that lender's services. A wise seller's agent asks a lender of his choice to confidentially approve the buyer, even if the buyer will eventually use a different lender. This way, the seller and seller's agent, though they never personally review the buyer's confidential information, know the likelihood that the deal will go through.*

Ann calls Brad and tells him to contact her friend Lenny, a loan broker. Brad calls Lenny, and they agree that Brad will use Lenny for the loan. Lenny faxes to Ann a loan pre-approval.

An agent cannot insist the buyer use his friend to obtain a loan. There are big differences between lenders, and buyers should check them out themselves. In most, perhaps all, jurisdictions, a loan broker cannot pay the agent a commission. There is, however, no way to track what cash or gifts may be handed over when no one is watching. The costs of the other services are relatively low, but a loan broker can make very large profit.

Sally and Brad sign the contract and send copies to the designated escrow office. The escrow officer assigned to the transaction writes up the instructions. Both Abe's and Ann's offices will start verifying that all the disclosures are signed.

Because of the nuisance of lawsuits over the years, the stack of paperwork is gigantic. It would be unreasonable to think the principals could actually read all of it. Some of the disclosures are so foolish as to warn the buyer that rain may cause the property to become wet.

The **inspections** are scheduled to check over the house. The home inspector comes out and, as it is his job to do, finds every little thing wrong with the house that he can. Brad looks over the long report and notices nothing major, but decides he can use it to demand that Sally either fix every loose screw or give him a discount in the selling price.

I find this very annoying, unless there is a code violation or an expensive repair the seller neglected to mention. No one likes his or her things to be disparaged. The seller will become upset with the buyer and that animosity will last for the full escrow period. Once a buyer has insisted on an $800 discount for a carpet stain he saw before he made the purchase offer, the seller is less likely to cooperate on anything else. I once had a deal fall through because each principal insisted the other pay for a $2 piece of PVC needed on the hot tub. Each would not let anyone pay for it but the other principal.

Sally and Brad get together and decide that, rather than either one of them paying to fix the roof, they will bluff the agents so that if the agents don't pay for the repairs, they will cancel the deal. After all, they say to each other, "Those agents are getting overpaid for their work." Sally and Brad agree that Abe and Ann will each give them $1,000 from the commission.

It will never stop amazing me how some people rationalize away their obligations, their responsibilities, and their loyalties when it comes to money. Yes, the brokers will be dividing $24,000 for their work. But the agents only get part of that (maybe as low as 50%) because their broker's offices will take a big split to cover overhead. Between the time they spent and the money they advanced out of pocket, the agents are likely getting about $6,000 each after costs on this deal. If you include all the deals they spent time and money on that did not go through, you will find they are usually barely making a living. On rare occasions, if the agent did not follow an agreement or was acting as a "double agent," it may be fair to reduce the commission.

Meanwhile, Lenny the loan broker has been working on the loan for Brad. Lenny has promised an attractive interest rate that seems so low that Brad decides not to look around for a better deal.

Loan brokers often promise what they know they cannot give in order to lock the buyer in. There are requirements that the lender give a **truth in lending** *disclosure, but all the loan broker has to do to get out of it is find the client "not eligible" for that loan. The loan broker switches the buyer to a worse loan after it is too late for the buyer to shop around for better deals.*

The loan broker then informs Brad of the loan he is qualified for, but tells him that there are "**points**."

This is the loan broker's fee for working for you. Each point is one percent of the loan amount. Though the whole reason to hire a loan broker is to get the best deal possible, the loan broker is motivated to get the buyer the worst loan he can. The loan broker's office will then add small fees for such things as loan review and processing. This can become very expensive, but it is the way it works. Not all loan brokers are deceptive, but the profit is high and the client has no way of knowing the breakdown of expenses. With that type of motivation, many loan brokers are tempted to put their profits above their morals.

Let's put greedy Lenny's profit all together now, using Brad's loan as an example. Brad buys the house for $400,000 and pays 20% with his own money as a down payment. The loan is for $320,000. Lenny charges Brad 2 points for his services, which is $6,400. The FI pays Lenny 3 points for giving Brad a lousy loan with a three-year prepayment penalty, which is $9,600. Lenny's office sneaks in about $2,000 in fees. Lenny therefore made $18,000 for acting as a middleman on the loan. With that much profit from only a few actual hours of work, a lot of people went into the loan business during the escalated home prices in 2002 - 2007. With some states allowing loan origination licensing through their Departments of Corporations as well as their Departments of Real Estate, it allowed an influx of loan brokers who were not as educated or experienced and who were not bound by the regulations that had protected buyers before. The higher kickbacks from the FIs inspired loan agents to give homebuyers lousy loans that escalated in interest rate.

Not all loan brokers charge so much and give such bad loans. Then again, some charge much more. In rare instances where the clients may require a lot of work or are extremely difficult to place, if the loan broker has to fix the buyer's credit, fish through boxes in the buyer's garage to find the paperwork, or shop the loan to dozens of FIs before finding one that will lend to the buyer's bad credit or situation, then perhaps the loan broker deserves his profits. But plenty of other brokers simply take the order, never talk to the client, have all the paperwork done by their office, spend only a few hours on the deal, and make just as much. If you have ever wondered why some loan brokers drive better cars than you or your real estate broker, this is why.

If your finances and credit are good enough that you can get a loan with decent rates and terms from the FI directly, there is no need to risk the deal the loan broker would give you. You should go direct.

Lenny calls an appraiser so that he can verify to the FI that the house has sufficient value to loan money against. The appraiser goes out to the house and takes measurements and pictures, then checks surrounding sales to find what other houses have been selling for using the "market approach" to finding value (discussed later). Any additions to the house that were not permitted are invisible to the appraiser and not used in consideration.

What you don't usually hear is that the loan broker tends to tell the appraiser what the sales price of the house is and the appraiser does his best, within mathematical limits, to match that price. The FI will also check over the appraisal to see if it is too far out of line. Sometimes the FI will "cut" the appraisal down, forcing the buyer to either come up with more money or have a larger Loan to Value (LTV). Example: Brad wants to borrow $320,000 to buy a $400,000 home, thus 80% LTV. But the FI cut the appraisal down to $380,000. Brad is given a choice of getting the $320,000, which will be an 84.2% LTV at a higher interest rate because of the FI's greater risk factor, or else getting an 80% LTV based on $380,000, which is only $304,000, meaning that Brad needs to come up with $16,000 more in cash.

Lenny's office has been working to get all of Brad's paperwork completed, and finally submits the information to the FI that will actually fund the loan. The FI assigns an **underwriter** to the account. The underwriter decides whether he sees anything that does not look right under the parameters of the FI requirements. The underwriter looks for things such as proof that a self-employed buyer really has a business and proof that the buyer is paying his share of the LTV with his own money, as well as credit report problems and other red flags. The underwriter submits a list of things he wants verified to Lenny.

Most loan brokers are honest with their submitted documents, though you will find some willing to risk jail time by creating fraudulent documents to avoid cancelling a deal. If the loan broker can't directly comply with the underwriter's requests, he will try to find a workaround: maybe all that is needed is a letter explaining why there is a slight discrepancy in the reports. If the FI refuses the loan, the loan broker may transfer the loan to a different FI with less stringent requirements about whatever the problem is, and that change may affect the interest rate.

Meanwhile, one week before the closing date, Sally wants to verify that the deal will close so that she can pack and move. Sally's agent Abe has been calling the escrow company trying to get confidential information on whether the FI has approved Brad for the funds.

This is sweat time! All parties are worried whether the deal will go through. All are spending money and taking actions with no guarantee that they will see anything for it. Inexperienced agents approaching the close of a deal sometimes believe money will be soon be coming in, and spend that money before they have it. If they have, this is the time when they panic. Phone calls, letters, and faxes fly back and forth threatening lawsuits if others do not perform on the deal.

Lenny is complying with the requests of the underwriter as fast as he can, but the underwriter's office takes a day or two to respond on whether each document is acceptable.

Most FI employees are diligent in their work. However, some underwriters, who make about $15 per hour, know the loan broker's profits and feel no sympathy when they make him wait a little longer before reviewing his files.

The date the deal was to close has passed when Lenny finally gets the FI to commit to fund the loan. However, it is not the original program Brad had agreed to, and when Brad is informed of the increased interest rate, he objects and starts calling all the other loan brokers he can find.

Countless times I have honestly told a person I can get them a certain rate but lost them to someone promising something I felt was impossible. Those people often call me after their closing date has passed and tell me their loan broker is now charging them more than I had offered and want me to give them what I told them I could—but there is no way to give instant loans. I tell them they are stuck with either taking the bad offer or losing their deposit and the house.

The FI has sent the documents Brad needs to the escrow office. Lenny sets up a time for Brad to sign them with a notary present to go through them with him. A "three day right of recession" may be in effect, where the documents are not valid until three days after signing.

Loan brokers prefer not to be in the room when the borrower signs because the borrower may ask why he did not receive what was promised. A borrower should insist that the loan broker be present.

Escrow will send a notice to the county recorder that Brad is the new owner of the house, that all of Sally's debts against the house have been paid, and that Brad now owes the new FI for the loan. In most jurisdictions, one day will pass to verify that no one recorded anything contrary to the agreement before escrow will give title or disburse funds.

The deal is done. Escrow "closes" and sends out the correct funds and paperwork to the right people. Brad owns the house and may move in as soon as he wants. Everyone is paid. Lenny buys season tickets to Ann's favorite ballet and gives them to Ann for having referred Brad to him and to insure that she will do the same in the future.

I know I said this previously, but it is important enough to say again. Loan brokers may not pay agents commissions for referrals, but they have many ways of sidestepping this. Sometimes they say that the real estate agent "assisted" the loan broker in completing the paperwork and it is not a referral but only a payment for services rendered. Many real estate offices now have in-house loan brokers, and the agent might receive a higher percentage of the sales commission if the principal uses the in-house lender. There are several other ways for the agent to get commission from the loan, including cash and "gifts." No reputable real estate agent should object to a principal receiving bids from other lenders.

Many deals go more smoothly than this one did, but many others go less well. Principals in real estate transactions need to keep an eye on who is working for them and what they are doing. When big money changes hands, many different people find different ways of scraping some off the top. In addition to simply losing money, if things go wrong through dishonesty or incompetence and the person at fault was working on behalf of the principal, the principal could be legally responsible.

I have told you about several different ways in which the people helping you may be dishonest or incompetent so that you understand what to watch out for. The truth is that most of the people you will meet are extremely knowledgeable and experienced. I once had a principal spend so much time calling everyone, checking over everything, and giving her "advice" that none of the very qualified people I had set up could get anything done for her. It is your right to request to be fully informed and updated, but do not harass your service providers. Many of them are superb at what they do.

What to Buy

You may not see all of your profit until you sell a property, but a great deal of that eventual profit is determined by how you buy.

There is an old story about a guy who is walking down the street when a middle-aged woman pulls up in a classic sports car. She tells the guy that she is getting a divorce because her husband left the state with his young secretary. The husband told her to sell his car and send him the profit from the sale. She tells the guy that she will sell him the car for $100 because that will be her revenge to her soon to be ex-husband.

In the above example, the sports car may have been worth $50,000, and because it is a classic it will increase in value in the years to come. We do not look at the guy's rate of return based on what the car was worth when he bought it, but rather what he paid, in this case only $100. The same is true with property: we find the rate of return based on the cost. The less paid, the greater the rate of return.

A helpful way to look at investments is to compare their value at the time of sale with the long-term profit. To make this clearer, let's assume you are offered two different 2-year contracted jobs that are equal in all respects except that one job will pay you an upfront bonus of $1,750, and the other will pay you a $2,000 bonus after 2 years. Which is the better deal? By calculating backwards with the average inflation rate of 3.5%, we find that $2,000 in 2 years has the buying power of $1,867 today, so it beats the $1,750. However, if you had $1,750 today and could invest it at 6.9% interest, you would have $2,000 in 2 years, equaling the other option. The answer to the question depends on whether you can invest the money at a better rate of return than 6.9%.

In this section, we will go over the methods that appraisers use to estimate value and how you can use them to know whether you have an outstanding deal on your hands. We will then go over what makes different areas increase in value and how to estimate which properties will become more profitable over time so that you can spot the better deals. Finally, we will talk about the different ways to find properties that are bargains either because they are low-priced or because of the upcoming appreciation in an area.

5.   Finding Value

Before making a profit on property, it is important to know what the value of the property is at the time that you purchase it. Sure, there are experts that will help determine this for you, but those experts don't come in until the deal is in escrow. You must know how much to offer for a property before the deal. It is also important to know what types of property to buy and in what areas. They say the three rules of real estate deals are: "location, location, location!" Location is certainly important, but sometimes the property in the best location is over-priced and a bad buy. On the other hand, a property in a bad location may have the highest opportunity to make a profit. A better three rules of real estate are: "strategy, opportunity, and timing."

The phrase "location, location, location" was first used by hotel owner Lord Charles Forte as a response to why one of his hotels was always booked full. But unless they're buying a place for a business, "location" is way down the list of importance for investment professionals. These ideas will become clearer when I explain the flow of property value later on. For now, let's use a few quick examples. A mansion in Beverly Hills is a great location, but because of the demand for that location, the price has already adjusted, and the appreciation of that property may be slow. A shabby barn in a bad neighborhood is the worst location, but for the person who buys it cheaply, knocks it down to build apartment buildings, and then sells it again, it may make a very fast profit. It could be that both properties will increase 8% per year, but there will more likely be other factors that influence how they appreciate.

People often ask me what a property is worth or whether something is a good deal. Even if I am relatively familiar with the area, I can't make an intelligent guess without spending time checking the area's recent history of sales. Inexperienced buyers use their emotions about the attractiveness of a property to value it. They don't take into consideration the fact that when they sell it, the eventual buyer will likely use math. Agents will try to influence emotional buyers. Recently, I had an agent tell me the property had the largest yard on the block. She failed to mention that all properties were the same size and this one simply had a smaller house. I have seen buyers be attracted to a property because of the "vibe," or some other factor that had little to do with the value or the use. Before you start to look, you need to decide whether you are looking for the perfect home despite slow increase in value, an investment, or something in between.

There are three recognized methods of appraising property: the **market approach**, the **replacement approach,** and the **income approach**. The market approach is the one most used for evaluating residential homes, so I will begin with a detailed explanation of it before describing the other two. Additionally, some land comes with a business already established on it, which you buy along with the property. I will therefore also explain how to evaluate **business opportunities** at the end of the chapter.

The **market approach** is the one most used in valuing single family residences (SFRs). The value of a property is simply what someone is willing to pay for it, and you can estimate that value by comparing a given property to similar property sold recently. You don't need to be an expert, but I will show you how to get reasonably close to the value and not make some common mistakes.

The first step is to find a source (or several sources) of information about recent sales. You can usually find the most accurate information in the county recorder's records, but most areas do not organize this for you. The local Multiple Listing Service (MLS) used by real estate agents is also a good source for this information and has the added advantage of displaying homes not yet sold and how long they have been on the market. Note that the MLS information is entered by the agent and not verified and therefore cannot be guaranteed correct.

There are also websites popping up like Zillow.com, Trulia.com, Redfin.com, Home.com, Realtor.com, and others, which offer listing information for free. They even do the math for you and estimate the value. Websites of this kind are constantly appearing, and new ones may have been developed between the time I'm writing this and the time you're reading it. You can find them by typing the address of the property you're interested in into a search engine and seeing what websites come up. Although these are great for a quick guess, they are often months behind and incorrect for a variety of reasons. If you are reviewing a large condominium building with similar units and a lot of recent sales or a housing development with houses all the same size, their calculations can be almost exact. But in other cases, not only may the information entered be factually inaccurate, but the programs cannot take into account factors that influence buyer demand. These programs, for instance, do not understand that the cost and demand for swimming pools in Wisconsin is different than it is in Arizona, or that one property may have a beautiful view its neighbors do not. Nor can they distinguish between the price of houses in a wealthy neighborhood and the houses in a poor neighborhood when the two are only a block away from each other. Remember also that these websites calculate based on the prices paid for property, not the real values. Sometimes there are deals behind the scenes, such as those between relatives or in foreclosures, where a property transfers title for a price very different from its value. If one property went for a dramatically different price than the others, examine it more carefully. If you can't explain the discrepancy, remove it from your calculations. I recommend entering the property you are interested in into all of the websites of this type that you can find: their information and their algorithms can be different from each other, and that can give you more information. These websites are a good starting point, but don't base your investments solely on their advice.

Always verify your information and draw your own conclusions before you buy. We will need to look at this from the appraiser's point of view. In the following section, I will show you how.

The appraiser gathers the most recent sales in the area for comparable properties (**comps**), usually those sold within the last 6 months. Let's say there are 5 houses sold that qualify as being similar, and we will call them A, B, C, D, and E. Unless we are looking at the same housing development or a condo project where all homes are exactly the same, even the most similar buildings will have differently sized land and/or buildings, as well as other factors such as pools and views. The appraiser takes the sale prices of the most similar properties and adjusts them to the "subject property" (property we are appraising). This means that we begin with the value of a recently sold property, subtract from it the value of any advantages the sold property has over the subject property, and add any advantages the subject has over the sold. By doing this, we have made two dissimilar properties similar enough to estimate what the person who bought the sold property may have been willing to pay for the subject property.

Here is an example of actually valuing a property with the market approach. Let's say that the subject property is 1,500 square feet, has no view, and does have a pool.

Property "A" sold for $400,000 and has 2,000 square feet of living area. Like the subject property, it has a swimming pool and no view. Dividing the square footage into the price, we find the person that bought property "A" was willing to pay $200 per square foot for the house. Since the subject property is only 1,500 square feet, the appraiser deducts $200 times 500 square feet to find that the value the buyer would have likely paid for the subject property is $100,000 less than property "A," or $300,000.

This may be confusing, so let's review without the math. The appraiser took a recently sold property and adjusted it to be the same square foot dimensions as the subject property to get a price. If a person would pay $10 for 10 candies, then it is likely they would still have paid $7 for 7 candies. House "A" was reduced the same way.

Property "B" is 1,500 square feet and has the exact same floor plan and age as the subject property. It sold for $300,000. However, it does not have a pool. The appraiser checks and finds that houses with pools in the area are selling for $15,000 more than houses without pools. The appraiser simply adds the value of the pool to what was paid to adjust property "B" to $315,000.

Again, we are changing the price of the house sold to be more like the one we are appraising. If a person would pay $10 for 10 candies, but a better-tasting candy costs $1.10 a piece, then it is likely the person would have spent $11 for 10 of the better-tasting candy.

The appraiser adjusts all the other recently sold properties in this manner. A large disparity in the numbers means the appraiser needs to look more closely, and if he cannot explain a selling price, he excludes it. After averaging the adjusted prices, the appraiser has a good estimate of what the buyers in that area would have been willing to pay for the subject property during the last six months.

One problem with this approach is that when homes are sold, they go into escrow for a month or two before the sale is official and goes on record. If the market is changing quickly enough, this causes a lag in the estimates: it will not reflect the new values of homes. The appraiser therefore checks the properties that are on the market but not yet sold to gage supply and demand and check whether he needs to adjust the price. If he finds there are more homes than normal on the market and few are selling, then the market is dropping. If there are few homes on the market and more than usual are selling, the area is increasing in value. Appraisals are never perfectly accurate, but with this approach, the appraiser arrives as close as possible to the value people may be willing to pay for the subject property.

Real estate agents wishing to save themselves time often use the prices at which properties are listed to guess the value of a property. This is wrong. The price unsold properties are listed at is only a good indication of what has not yet found a buyer—perhaps because they are priced too high. There may be ten homes for sale, all about the same size and listed for $500,000, but they have been sitting for 9 months with no one willing to buy them. All this tells us is that these homes are not selling for $500,000 and are worth something less than that amount.

On the other hand, we may see a large number of houses listed at $400,000 that seems to be selling as soon as they are listed. The problem here is that an ethical listing agent will not release the amount the house sold for until escrow closes. If the deal failed to close, the agent would have announced how much the seller was willing to sell for, harming future negotiations with a new buyer. For all we know, buyers may be offering more than the listed amount because of demand excitement in the area. Homes listed, homes sold, and the amount of time it has been taking to sell can give an indication of the movement of housing prices, but they don't tell us the value.

Appraisal is not an exact science, but rather a best estimate of what a buyer may be willing to pay. Even qualified appraisers with years of education and experience can come up with widely varying values. However, you can pick a neighborhood where you are interested in investing, do a market approach calculation every month or two, and have a basic idea what homes are selling for based on square footage, age, and amenities. With this knowledge, you will know instantly when a property is offered at a bargain price, and you can toss out preliminary offers to buy after only a minute of calculations. You may not know exactly what the appraiser would come up with after hours of work, but if you determine, based on your area knowledge, that the home is worth

$400,000, offering $350,000 would leave you plenty of room to get a good deal.

You may ask, "What if I offer $350,000 and later find out the home is worth only $325,000 because I miscalculated?" When you make your offer, you have the right to inspect the home and, within a certain time period, are allowed to change your mind at your own discretion. After you make an offer, go home and recheck your math, or have an appraiser check it out. If it is not the deal you want, you cancel.

The **replacement approach** becomes necessary when we do not have enough information to use another approach. If the property does not make income, then the income approach cannot work. If the property is unusual for the area or no similar properties have sold recently to show what people are paying, we cannot use the market approach. Imagine you are trying to sell the only log cabin in a rural area. How do you value it? Take the value of similarly zoned land in the area, then figure out what a contractor would charge to build the existing buildings. Reduce that amount based on depreciation (age and wear of the property) to come to a value. In our above example, assume that vacant land the same size as the log cabin property is selling for $200,000. It will cost $100,000 to build a log cabin, and the log cabin has decreased in value $30,000 because of age.

($200,000 + $100,000 - $30,000 = $270,000 value)

With the **income approach** to valuing property, we look at the income produced on the land. This approach is useful for commercial property, including apartments, retail stores and shopping centers, restaurants, hotels, medical centers, farms, and industrial property. It is almost never relevant for a SFR. Using a formula called Capitalization Rate (cap rate), we translate the cost of the property into the percentage of return on investment. Cap rate takes the Gross Operating Income (all income minus all expenses except loan debt) divided by the selling price of the property. This ratio tells you how many years it will take to make your investment back before you own the property outright and can make a profit. A cap rate of .10 (10%) means that a building pays 10% of its value each year, and so it will take 10 years for the building to pay for itself, not counting the interest that accrues on the loan debt. A cap rate of .05 (5%) means that it will take 20 years. Depending on the condition of the area and the building, it generally takes about 7 to 11 years to regain the invested capital.

We will now discuss how to value **business opportunities**. This can be very important to know because the sales of many commercial buildings include the businesses in them, which add to the total value. If you are not dealing with the sale of commercial property, feel free to skip to the beginning of the next chapter.

People spend years studying all the factors that determine the value of businesses, but unless you are planning on buying a multimillion-dollar business, you will not need to hire an expert. You can determine a sufficiently accurate value based on the information here and a little investigation of your own.

First, you will need to understand the "valuation multiplier," which equals the amount of time it will take for the new business owner to earn back the value of his investment, similar to the calculations we used for the income approach above. To illustrate how and why this number can vary, here are some examples.

I know of professional-looking pool service people that go door to door to pick up clients. These people are knowledgeable and offer to work for one week free to prove their skills. After a week of spectacular work, the pool service person enter into a contract with the homeowner for monthly service, generally for higher than the normal rate. The service person immediately sells the contract to someone else for a price equal to two months' wages. The first service person made two months' pay for one week's work. The new person who bought the contract will work for two months for free but has made a client who could last for years and who might never realize that the expert stopped working there. (These types of services are normally done when the homeowner is at work.) If, however, the homeowner was home one day and looked out the window at the wrong moment, the new business owner might lose the business even before those two months were up. The homeowner might find out the business was sold but like the new service man anyway, but the new service man has no way of knowing that in advance. The risk factor of buying this contract is high, and so the new business owner would not buy it if it took more than a couple of months working for free before he made a profit. Therefore, the seller charges based on a "valuation multiplier" of two months. The seller decided, and the buyer (by buying) agreed, that the business is worth two months of income.

Compare this to a dental office that has had the same clientele for ten years. If another dentist buys the business, assuming he is as competent as the old one, very few patients will leave. Because of the quality of the clients and the reputation of the business (this reputation for quality is known as "goodwill"), the new dentist may be willing to buy with a valuation multiplier of four years or more, meaning that he works for four or more years before he sees a profit. The dentist who sold the business he spent all those years building gets paid up-front the profit he would have made over those next four years.

Different types of businesses have different risk factors and therefore different valuation multipliers, and the length of establishment also adds a percentage to the value. There are two basic starting points to calculating the value of a business. If the business is product sales or a very stable income like a gas station or insurance business, multiply net sales by a multiplier that will usually be between 1.5 and 2.5 years. If the business is more service-oriented, multiply the profit (more accurately called "expendable income") by a multiplier usually between 2 and 6 years. The multiplier varies for types of businesses and by location. A full calculation of the value must consider other factors, such as expected growth in profit and accounts receivable and payable. The valuation multipliers change constantly and differ by area, but a list is available to purchase online for about $50.

As a buyer, you do not necessarily need to look up the recommended valuation multiplier, and can instead calculate the multipliers that business owners have chosen to use and compare them. Check the prices of similar businesses in the area and calculate the owners' yearly profits. If one shoe store's asking price will take 3 years to pay for itself, and the one down the block will take 2.7, then the second one is asking for a better price. Before you spring for the bargain, however, you might want to look into exactly what makes the first owner judge his business to be less risky than the second one does. This comparison between years of profit and asking price is the valuation multiplier, and it's a useful way to compare one business to another.

This all may sound complicated, so let's work through calculating the value of a barbershop. Imagine we are considering buying "Happy Cuts," a barbershop in a mall. People often try to sell businesses on leased land when their leases are expiring, leaving the new owner a business to run and nowhere to run it. Therefore, first we verify that the lease has time

54

on it and, hopefully, options to extend the lease. The rest is all comparatively easy mathematics. Take the Gross Profit (all money made in a year) minus the expenses to run the business, and you will know what the Net Profit is for that year. It is best to have at least three years of records.

Another important thing to check is whether the owner has been paying himself for time managing the business or whether he did the work for free. After all, you don't want to buy a job, but a profit-making machine. Even if you plan on running the business yourself, your time has monetary value and this is an enormous difference in the calculation. If there was not a paid manager and you will either have to pay one or do it yourself, subtract the value of the owner's time from the supposed net profit to arrive at the real net profit. For example, if the owner worked all year long for free and it would cost $40,000 per year to hire someone to replace him, deduct that amount from the yearly Net Profit.

Now we have a true Net Profit. If you have found out the accepted valuation multiplier for the business type in advance, multiply that value by the true Net Profit. Add to that the cost of used equipment and supplies to get a reasonable asking price. If you do not wish to buy the list of valuation multipliers, you can simply find the valuation multiplier the seller chose. First, figure out a reasonable value to buy the used equipment and subtract that from the asking price. Now divide the asking price (minus equipment) by the profit to get the seller's valuation multiplier.

Happy Cuts income statement:

Gross income	$220,000
Expenses	- $120,000
Net profit	$100,000
Cost to pay a manager	- $40,000
True Net Profit	$60,000
Used equipment and any supplies	$20,000
Asking price	$200,000
Asking price – Equipment	$180,000
Valuation Multiplier	3 years

The current owner is asking $200,000 for Happy Cuts. We subtract the value of the equipment ($20,000) from the sales price to arrive at $180,000 for the actual business. Dividing that by the $60,000 true Net Profit, we find it will take 3 years of making the $60,000 true Net Profit to fully pay off the investment and to start making a profit ourselves. At the end of those 3 years, you have your $180,000 investment back and now own a business worth $180,000. You have doubled your money in 3 years, which is an interest rate of about 26%. At the beginning of the 4th year, you are now making money.

Now that we have reduced the price of a business to time and interest return on investment, we can calculate the value of other barbershops in the same way and compare them to find out what shop is the best value for your money.

Note: I removed the equipment from the math in our example because a barbershop is a mostly service business. When comparing the value of different opportunities, we generally remove equipment and supplies from the equation. However, for a business that is more supply-related, such as a retail store, the equipment would have been kept in the equation to figure return on investment.

In a recent conversation with several Business Opportunities agents, they informed me that the current trend is not to use the value of equipment at all, since the equipment is required to make the profit. I find difficulty with this trend. Let's say someone owns a website that makes $100,000 per year with no company-owned equipment. Now assume someone else owns a $400,000 crane and rents it out for $100,000 per year. Per the Business Opportunities agents, (assuming both are valued at a multiplier of three years times the true Net Profit) both companies would have the same selling value of $300,000… and yet $300,000 wouldn't even buy you the crane!

6.   Highest and Best Use

Now that you know how to appraise property, the next important considerations are the growth of appreciation in an area and the highest and best use of the property you will be buying. We do not have a crystal ball to see what the future will bring, but by using logic and reviewing the concepts of market movement, we can make very good estimates.

You want, first of all, a location that works for your goals. You also want to get the best deal on it that you can get. Sometimes you will do this by foreseeing market changes before the seller does. Sometimes you will find a seller willing to take a reasonable loss in order to get on with his life. That loss is your profit! There are a few more concepts you will need to know in order to know a deal when you see it. We will go over **supply & demand**, **diminishing returns**, and **speculated increases**. Even if you have some knowledge of these concepts already, you should read on to see how they apply to market movement and valuation. Finally, we will talk about the value of future money and how to translate it into today's money to determine what payment plans are best for you.

What is the best location?
We need to look at where we want to buy property. This varies greatly, of course, depending on your needs and intentions for the property. Someone planning to retire in a home is looking for something different than someone planning to fix up a house for a quick resale and a profit. This can drastically change what type of properties you will be looking for and what area you want.

All real estate is local. This means that events going on five miles away may not impact a property at all. If you try to research all areas at once, it will take up all of your time. Instead, find the area that fits your purposes best, then calculate the basic value of that area and watch for the right deal.

History teaches us that a neighborhood has a life cycle of its own.

Imagine properties at a particular place and time being utilized for their "highest and best use." Later, the properties age, the needs of the community change, and the properties decline in value. Landlords scoop up the homes to rent them out to lower-income people, and instead of a neighborhood of owners we have a neighborhood of tenants. When the properties become cheaper than surrounding areas, investors purchase them and refurbish them to the new highest and best use.

Let's look at an example. We talked earlier about developers buying farmland. Now we will look at how that land will be used and how the price changes over time.

A developer buys cheap, raw land a mile from town. The developer builds a housing tract, and the value for that land jumps. Wealthy families buy up and live in the new houses, attracting other wealthy families that wish to live near others in their own socioeconomic class, causing the property to appreciate at higher than the average rate. After a time, the houses become old and their amenities grow outdated. Their lack of the current advancements in living needs (eg. low electrical power, lack of the newest cable needs, improper use of living area like few bathrooms, etc.), causes the appreciation rate to decrease. Newer housing developments spring up around the neighborhood and attract buyers away from the now older housing tract. The original tract homes stagnate in appreciation. The people who live there are older, and many of them care for their properties less well. Many owners move to better neighborhoods and rent their properties to tenants. The prices of these houses may never have dropped—there may even always have been some appreciation—but compared to the higher-priced newer homes, these houses are a bargain. Middle-income families can afford to buy or rent in the area, and the prices become even more stagnant. The new tenants and owners may lack the funds or desire to keep their homes painted and maintained.

Small-time investors see profit in the neighborhood. Maybe the houses are large and can be divided into small apartments to make more rental income. Maybe the properties simply need to be cleaned up with superficial cosmetic changes to bring them up to standard. Perhaps major changes, such as adding a second floor or other additions, will greatly increase the demand and therefore the value. If the present use is far enough from the highest and best use, it may be cheap enough for a buyer to buy the land, tear down the current building, and build something that fits the current needs and demand. Whatever the circumstances, the once falling-apart neighborhood will again grow to its highest and best use. Over many years, investors will buy the cheap homes and improve or rebuild them, once again attracting wealthier families willing to pay top dollar. Later, these upper-class families will move away to areas that suit them better. Home values will fall, and the cycle will start over.

The point of this example is that, although the properties were appreciating throughout the process at rates better than inflation, there were periods where the prices rose more quickly. It benefits the buyer to buy at the right time. If you determine that an area is not going to grow substantially in value, it is better to look in another area because it may be many years before an area changes.

You can determine the phase of rise or decline by reviewing the appearance and history of the neighborhood. Look up the ages of the homes. Drive through the surrounding streets to check the average upkeep to figure out whether the houses are owned or rented. Drive around late on Friday and Saturday nights to see whether undesirables are hanging out drinking beer on their car hoods. Look for current or recent construction or filed permits to see whether investors have become interested in the neighborhood.

You will need to determine what phase of rise or decline best suits your needs. If you want a home to stay in for a long time, you will want to buy as the neighborhood rises in value. If you want a good deal and a quick resale, you will buy near the top of the rise. If your buying power is limited, you may want to buy as the neighborhood values drop and plan on holding the property for a few years until investors become interested in the area. If you want to invest, and have the funds to improve the property, you'll buy after the neighborhood has reached rock bottom.

Price = Supply & Demand
There are ways to get property at a reduced value, but before we can beat the system, we need to understand how prices move. The theory of supply and demand states that if a lot of people want a product, the cost of the product goes up. Once the supply of the product has increased over the demand, the price goes down. Let's look at an example.

Let's say someone invents a car that goes 100 miles on a gallon of gas, and a company manufactures 1,000 of those cars. Because of lack of promotion, few know of the cars and fewer buy them. There is no demand yet for the product. The company lowers the price to move the cars because they have too much supply. National news broadcasts announce that this innovative car has been proven reliable, and demand skyrockets to well beyond the 1,000 available. The company raises the price to what people are willing to pay. They build cars as fast as they can, foreseeing an endless number of buyers. The supply equals the demand and the price evens out. But now, a competing company comes out with a car that goes 120 miles per gallon! Because of public demand and a still-small supply, the 120 mile car company can overprice these cars. The 100 mile car company drops their price to catch the business from those who can't afford the overpriced 120 mile cars. When the supply of 120 mile cars increases to meet the demand, the price falls to something more affordable, and the 100 mile cars have to drop further in price. In time, companies come out with 140 mile cars and the 100 mile car company lowers the price (maybe even under their cost to make them), hoping to sell off those 100 mile cars they have left in stock.

A good real-world example was the Betamax recording machines. In the 1980s, they were such a new concept that they cost over $1,000 in 1980 dollars. Then VHS came out with a recording machine that sold at $800, and the Betamax dropped to compete. VHS dropped again, and then Betamax dropped, and so on. By the time VHS won the war, Betamax was selling below the cost of production just to get them off the shelves. If we translated these prices to today's dollars, taking into consideration the buying power of over 30 years ago, a VHS machine today should cost over $2,000. So many companies make VHS machines, however, that you can buy for $80 something ten times as good as what you could have gotten 25 years ago. Now that DVDs, CDs, computer downloads and cable optics all use High Definition digital and Blu-ray, VHS is becoming as hard to find as the old 8-track tape players, and VHS machines sell at garage sales for a few bucks. With the current breakthroughs in wireless Internet and the instant gratification we can now get simply by touching a screen, all forms of video ownership may soon drop in value, making people wonder why they ever stood in line to buy them.

Now let's apply this concept to "raw, unimproved land" (land with little or nothing built on it). Assume there are 500 acres of raw land 100 miles from any road, and all the property has is a fence around it. No one wants this raw land because no one can use it. There is plenty of supply and very little demand, so the value is low. But a road is built nearby. People begin to use the land for camping, hunting, farming, etc. With more demand, the value of the land increases slightly. Then a general store is built nearby: again, an increase. As the area becomes a town and then grows into a city of thousands of people, speculators foresee eventual value in the land and the price increases. The city announces the construction of an airport or some major industrial improvements, and investors speculate on the increased demand, creating growth in value. The city improves the land to be ready for available water, power, and sewage, and now the land is ripe to be built into housing. The land is now too expensive for any one developer to buy the whole 500 acres, so the owner subdivides it into smaller portions. More developers can afford the smaller 100-acre parcels, bringing more buyers and a higher price per acre than the owner could have asked while selling the whole 500. The developers now bring sewage, electrical, and water right up to each individual housing lot, and the price jumps again. The developers subdivide their 100 acres into 400 quarter-acre lots and build homes. Most families would rather buy homes than improve land, so demand from prospective homeowners rises. Investors buy up and improve the surrounding area and build a shopping center down the road. The homes are now convenient for jobs and shopping, creating more demand. However, if other builders build better or cheaper homes on other land near these properties, the demand may fall and the value may go down.

Diminishing Returns
Let's look at attic insulation. In an attic with no previous insulation, adding an inch of insulation saves on heating costs. After you get to the thickness that is recommended (let's say 8 inches in this case), maybe 90% of the heat stays in the house. Adding 8 more inches of insulation can't save another 90%, but perhaps it will help us retain another 5% of the total heat. If we add to this 16 inches of insulation another 8 inches, it improves the heat retention so little that you might as well not have done it. The cost for the first 8 inches received good value in heating savings, the next 8 probably cost more to install then the savings could ever be, and adding any more is an outright waste of money. This is called diminishing returns.

A property that has been built grossly bigger than the other homes in the area may not have the most value per square foot because there's no demand for that monstrosity among people who buy in that location. On the other hand, the greatest profit can be from bringing a small house up to meet the needs of the area. We will be talking about this in more detail later on, but for now, understand that bringing a house to slightly above the standard in the area will usually get you the best return on your investment.

Speculated Increases
When valuing a property, remember that value depends not only on what something is now but also on what people believe it will become. In the stock market, if the government announces it will increase bridge building, the stock for cement companies goes up even before any contracts are made. Likewise, when the city near our currently difficult-to-reach property talks about building an airport, people will become more interested in our land. The closer the airport comes to completion, the more the land around it will go up in value. After the demand for land around the airport equals the supply, the appreciation rate will return to normal.

Now, let's use what we have learned to see how we can beat the theory and take advantage of the market movement. If you buy raw land in the middle of nowhere, you may make a profit for your great-grandchildren, but you likely won't see any returns yourself. If you follow a trend in demand that too many other people have already realized, you will be buying after the price has adjusted and make little profit.

Making money through speculation takes imagination and innovation. You will have to perceive the movement of demand based on the supply and move before the price increases. Let's say you find a house going for cheap because there is no shopping or jobs near it. You notice that some developers of shopping centers are buying up land in the area. When the stores are built a year later, the house you bought will jump in value. If you bought the house when it was cheap, you speculated successfully. As another example, let's say you find a high-demand area with a few plots of raw land and some run-down buildings. If you acquire this land before others notice the value, you can sell it for top dollar to others who wish to build something that conforms to the area. In the first example, we bought the property because we saw increasing demand, while in the second we bought the property because we saw decreasing supply.

Foreseeing price movements and increases in profit is important for a speculator, but understanding what you want property for and researching your intentions before buying is equally important. Many people hear of a "deal" and jump at it, even if it was not what they were looking for. Sure, some deals are so good they're worth further investigation. But it is a lot easier to decide what you want to do, find an area to do it in, and then learn everything there is to know about the area and your goals. If you know that, you will see the deals when they come and know what to do with them.

A friend once told me of a great deal that was not on the market yet. A gas station owner needed to move back to his native country to take care of his sick mother. The owner was willing to sell the gas station for almost half price to make the move quickly. Owning a gas station was never one of my interests, and I knew nothing about the area at all—but I couldn't walk away from this. I spent two solid weeks reviewing income documents and contracts with vendors, checking comparable gas stations, and sitting in my car across the street counting the customers. And then I came across a recently passed local ordinance that would make it a zoning violation to operate a gas station in that vicinity. The deal was dead and I was happy I did my homework, but it was a lucky escape. I often investigate very diversified investing, either for myself or for clients, so this was not unusual for me, but it was slightly outside my expertise. Even as equipped and experienced as I was, I still wasted a few weeks of my time. Had my research been any less thorough, I might even have missed those new zoning laws. Had I, on the other hand, been dealing with a region and a type of business I knew, I would have known about that ordinance before I'd even heard of the deal. The same goes for the average investor looking at a house: no matter what you are looking for, there is nothing like knowing the vicinity.

This is the mindset that will put you above the others that are competing for the deals in your community. If you become localized and specialized, you will know where prices will increase most. You will know the value of property. You will have done the math on how much it will cost you to fix, subdivide, cosmetically repair, or whatever your final intent is so that you know what your profit will be before you even knock on the potential seller's door. You will be able to make an offer while standing on the doorstep.

The Value of Future Money, Today.
In the old Popeye cartoons, there was a character named Wimpy who

often said, "I'd gladly pay you Tuesday for a hamburger today." This raises the burning question: "How much is a hamburger worth today if you don't have to pay for it until Tuesday?" Figuring out the long-term value of different choices can get confusing because it is hard to compare investments over different time frames. It goes back to the much older question: "which is more valuable, a bag of apples or a bag of oranges?" Unless there is a common denominator, this question cannot be answered. Luckily, we have the price listed in the grocery store as a common denominator to answer the apples and oranges question, and we have the "expected rate of return" to tell us how much a hamburger today is worth on Tuesday.

By taking the future value of an investment and expressing the amount in today's money, we can compare two very different investments to see which is better.

This is best showed in an example. Let's say we are fortunate enough to win $10 million tax free in the lottery. We are given the option of receiving all that money in payments over 26 years or cashing out for $5.8 million today. Which is a better deal?

With the payments, you will receive $384,615 each year, which is enough money to retire for life. You are also inspired to take the payments because it would be a shame to just toss away the extra $4.2 million by taking all that money up front. On the other hand, it would be great to have all that money in your bank right now. It's a tough call. But if we take the emotions out of it and leave it to the math, we can further investigate the proposal.

The first thing to ask is, based on an average inflation rate of 3.5% per year, what will that $384,615 last payment be able to buy 26 years from now? Using my financial calculator, it turns out that the buying power will be $157,245 on the last payment. In other words, the cost of products will have grown so that you will be able to buy with that money as much as $157,245 could in today's market. This is a lot of money, but it may not be up to the standard of living you got used to when you had the buying power of almost 400 thousand present-day dollars a year during the first few payments.

The next thing I did was pull out my handy dandy interest rate calculator again and determine what interest we would need to make on our $5.8

million to break even with the yearly payment plan. I found that we would need to make 5% interest. This is greater than the inflation rate of 3.5%, but not a great return on investment.

We have changed time into today's value for the money. The lottery offers us a choice between taking the $5.8 million today or letting them invest it for us at 5% interest, with periodic payments. The payments are over the estimated inflation rate, and even if the going rate of return falls, we will still have our rate of 5%. However, if the inflation rate skyrockets, or if the rate of return on investments becomes very high, we will not be able to direct our money into a higher interest-gaining investment. For example, if we could find a bond that paid only 1% more that 5%, we could still invest all that money, still receive all those monthly payments, and at the end of the 26 years still have $2,259,000 in the bank!

There are relatively stable "A" rated and very stable "AAA" rated companies offering bonds for rates requiring a 5, 10, or 20-year contract. These vary in the interest rates they offer depending on the current state of the economy, but the average over the last hundred years has been 6%. As I said in the beginning of the book, there is always some chance that a company will have financial troubles, but we are not locked in for 30 years, and the return is much greater than the percentage the Lotto is offering us. During good economic times, we could buy a bond with 9% interest, get the full lottery payment, withdraw amounts equal to the 26 yearly payments from our bank, and still have $15 million in the bank after 26 years.

Now we will make still better use of the money. Let's say we buy for cash (no leverage) a whole block of apartment buildings for our $5.8 million. When I described the income approach to appraisal, I described how we can calculate the investment returns on commercial buildings using the Capitalization Rate (cap rate) method. It is reasonable to expect to find a building investment that will pay itself back in about 10 years or less. If we make such an investment, we will make $580,000 per year in profit. However, unlike the yearly payments we were receiving from the Lotto, the rents in our building will increase with inflation, meaning that we will be earning not $580,000 a year, but *$580,000 a year in today's buying power*. The actual figure will increase with inflation and also figure into the increased appreciated price of the block in 26 years. We will have $580,000 to spend each year, and the $5,800,000 we invested is growing in value with the block of apartments we own.

If we go one easy step further, we can use leverage and only put 33% down on the properties, using our $5.8 million to buy three blocks with a total value of $17,400,000. Assume the interest rate on our loan with the FI (bank) is 7% and that it is fully amortized so that in 20 years we own the 3 blocks fully. After paying the FI, we would still have $711,559 left over each year to pay maintenance on the apartments. Each year, we raise our rents with the inflation rate, but our payment to the bank never goes up. After 20 years, we no longer need to make loan payments. At that point, we will be receiving the today's buying power equivalent of $1,740,000 each year to live on and own outright the inflated value of the three blocks of apartments, which even at only 3.5% growth will be $34,622,000 ($81,000,000 at 8% growth factor).

So what is a hamburger worth today if you don't have to pay for it until Tuesday? It all depends on how much return on investment you can make on the cost of a hamburger between now and Tuesday.

7.   Finding Properties

Now we can get into the meat of making profit in RE. You now know the terminology used in the industry, the way transactions work, how to value property, and where to look for property. You've probably seen those late-night commercials on real estate investment that talk about different ways to buy and handle property; I call them the "Midnight Infomercials." I will be using them as examples, so this is a good time to talk about what they teach and what they fail to teach.

Those **midnight infomercials** don't give you any new or exciting methods of doing business, just old ways looked at from different angles with more unrealistic hype than information. In the infomercials, person after person tells you how much money they made, supposedly using the program they want you to buy. But there's no independent verification, and even if the people speaking really did make some money, there's no way to verify that the program had anything to do with it. Sometimes the guy bragging about his profits is akin to the example of the guy who bought the ex-husband's classic car for $100: it may really happen, but not more than once a century. It would be silly to buy a book about how to stand on corners waiting for vengeful ex-wives in expensive cars, but that's more or less what these infomercials are. They can't tell you what their "plans" really are because then there would be no reason to buy their programs. Most of those plans can be explained in a few sentences, but they sell you books, videos and supposed contracts which "can be used anywhere." All they've shown you by the end is people standing in front of nice homes and fast cars towing faster boats, throwing money in the air, and all you have learned is that some people *say* they made money. Then the announcer either asks you to buy hundreds of dollars worth of books or to attend a free or cheap seminar that will tell you to spend thousands of dollars on a different course. Naturally, this thousand-dollar course is one that will finally tell you the big money-making secret.

Twenty-something years ago, as ashamed as I am now about it, I actually purchased one of those business plans for $100. I got 3 books for my money. All 3 books talked about how nice it was to be rich, how, by using their plan, I would be rich, and then, buried in repetitive hype, gave only the most vague financial advice. My money got me nothing but three monotonous books without a single business plan between them. A year later, I received a letter from the company offering me a free trip to sit in the audience of a new midnight infomercial they were about to film. They said that all I had to do was claim their plan worked. No one would ever check whether I had even tried the program. If I claimed I made a lot of money from their plan, they might pay me to appear in the commercial. When I see those people claiming they made money off a midnight infomercial, I wonder whether they are just the people who opted for the free vacation.

If it were really possible to work five hours a week and buy one house per month at $30,000 cash profit on closing, then the people making the seminars would hire someone to work 40 hours per week, buy 8 houses a month, pay the employee a $3,000 monthly salary, and keep $240,000 a month for themselves. Instead, they would rather sell you their starter plan for a few hundred and their advanced plan for $5,000. If they actually had a plan, they would be profiting off it themselves. If they were so magnanimous that they only wanted to help you make that profit, they wouldn't charge $5,000 to tell you how. This is about as ridiculous as paying a psychic to pick the winner of a horse race: if your psychic knew the winning horse, he would bet on it himself and not ruin his odds by telling you.

Buying at a profit can be done, but it is a lot of work. If you go into it knowing that it is work and are willing to put in the time and effort, you will find it to be the most profitable second job you will ever have. Eventually, it could be your only job.

When I was running my real estate company, I received a few calls a week from people asking questions that I knew they got from the midnight infomercials: "I am looking for an equity partner," "Do you know of any pre-foreclosures?" "Will any of your listings take a short sell?" One of my agents once took an offer to purchase a listed property from a guy that was going to pay with 30-year savings bonds, I killed that deal the moment I saw it. The only way to buy something for less than it is worth is to have someone else lose money in the sale. After the hype of making fast money wears off, most people realize the moral issues of wiping out someone else's life savings, whether or not the methods are technically legal.

[Note: Recieving 30-year government bonds to buy property at over full list price may sound good to the uneducated seller. The seller our office represented had listed their home for $270,000, and the buyer offered $300,000 in bonds! Sounds great, but those bonds are not cashable for 30 years from the purchase date. $300,000 in bonds could be purchased by the buyer at $150,000, and are worthless until 30 years from now. The seller would have to wait all that time to get today's value of their sold property, only making about 2% interest on the buyer's money. The buyer would have ripped the seller off for $120,000.]

We will go over situations where we can find people who are willing to lose profit on their property, people that don't understand the value of their property, and property where the price has yet to adjust to the supply and demand. I will not do as the midnight infomercials do and tell you this is easy. It is hard work and takes a lot of thinking and planning, but it can pay very well. Once you have a system working for you, it will very likely pay a lot more than your boss made at your normal job!

Everything worthwhile in the infomercials can be distilled down to one or two ideas. After the basics you've learned in the first section of this book, those ideas will only take a page or two to explain. I will tell you about the methods the midnight infomercials use that actually work and a few ideas that even they don't know. I will tell you the pitfalls to watch out for. I won't go into the minute-by-minute transaction, because the escrow company will do that for you once you have the deal. Finding the deal and negotiating the deal is all you need to know.

Some midnight infomercials claim to have "contracts that can be used in any state," but any reputable source will tell you that each state is so different that even a contract that is close to being right for your area's laws could still not be the best for your jurisdiction. Also, the laws change so fast in all the different jurisdictions that any such contract could be obsolete before it was printed. When you find a deal, go to the local Board of Realtors and buy at a slight premium price the most up-to-date contract for your state. Read it carefully and correct anything that doesn't apply to you (some sections only apply to members of the Board), and then add an addendum (an extra piece of paper that is referred to in the contract as being part of the contract) that states any additional information needed in the type of sale you have worked out.

Finding the right Seller

In the previous chapter, we talked about how to decide what you intend to do with a property. You now know in what area you want to buy and you have researched the going prices so you can spot a deal. You might find that deal in the MLS, on the Internet, or in a newspaper, but you will have competition (demand) because everyone else will see it too. We will now go over how to find the property others are not looking at yet.

The first thing to know in dealing with sellers is how to properly appraise their properties. We already talked about the basics of getting a close estimate, but if you don't feel comfortable making your own basic appraisal yet, it is best either to have a broker give you a Comparative Market Analysis (CMA) for a per-house fee, or pay a licensed appraiser for a desktop appraisal (quick computer-driven appraisal) for you, which normally costs about $50. Buying property is a big investment, so do your homework first and be willing to spend a few dollars now for profits later on. Always know the value of the property. This will tell you immediately whether the seller is asking something unreasonable or offering a good deal. As I said previously, do not value property by emotion, because the person who eventually buys from you will use math. I consider myself a moral person, but I don't see it as my duty to inform someone that they are asking too little for something I want to buy. (Unless I am also acting as a Broker in the deal: then there are legal and ethical issues.)

No matter how you find your seller that is willing to lose money on his home, your attitude when approaching him matters. Let me demonstrate this with a story. A loan broker friend of mine had been notified that a Notice of Default (NOD) had been filed against a $100,000 loan she had created two years before. The homeowners were not paying their bills. With some quick checking, I found that this elderly couple had tens of millions in stock from a major entertainment company and must have had the funds. Something was wrong! We went to their two-million-dollar house to find it rundown and overgrown. No one answered the front door, but we found a stack of letters hand-delivered by people who wanted to buy the property for cheap. We read through the offers. The thing they all had in common was that the letter-writers had all been writing from the perspective of how much they wanted to make off the distress of fellow human beings.

We spent an hour knocking at all the windows of the home to eventually find the old couple living in only one room. They were no longer able to care for themselves. Garbage was piled up literally waist high in the house, and there were rats running around. Someone willing to help them meet their goals and needs could buy this fixer-upper for a good price. These very sweet multi-millionaires needed help, and it was time for them to move to assisted living. The problem was, they wanted to stay in their home. I came up with an alternate plan to pay off their $100,000 loan, have a crew clean their home and put sufficient money in an account to give them a caregiver one day a week for five years, in exchange for a $500,000 paid-off vacation home they no longer needed and would never return to. The point I am making is that when someone has his back against a wall, he would rather deal with the person giving him a hand than with the person kicking him.

The Multiple Listing Service (MLS)

There are ways of looking deeper in the MLS than even most professionals know about in order to spot the deal you want. By searching the MLS, you can find homes that are listed as "fixers," "motivated sellers" or "REO" (Real Estate Owned, meaning owned by an FI). Sometimes the agent is only using these terms to get people interested in the property and increase demand, but sometimes these are the leads you need to find the home you can work with. Understand that demand will be higher for anything on the MLS because all agents can see it. But if you see an opportunity that others do not, it may be your deal.

Here is one way to think outside the box. Remember our discussion about diminishing returns and how the best value for your money comes from bringing a house into line with its neighborhood? If you are willing to build additions onto your property, the MLS can be a great tool to find a property where adding a room would make you a good profit. If you do it right, this is not as hard as it may seem. Most services allow an agent to check for properties under a variety of search methods, but very few buyers pay much attention to the "price per square foot." First, do a basic search of a neighborhood and find the average SF of the homes and the average price per SF that the homes have been selling for. Now, do a two-field search for homes. In the first field, search for homes starting at a little less than the average SF, and in the second field, search for a little lower than the average price per SF. List the results in order of lowest price per SF and work your way through. Think of each home in terms of what would make it desirable in the neighborhood. Look at the floor plans and make sure there's a place where your planned addition would work. There is much more on this later.

Door knocking

This may sound like grunt work, but it is not. If you have done your research on the neighborhood, you can introduce yourself door to door and talk about how you or your sister is thinking of buying a home in the area. Most people will be very kind, even if they have no intention of selling. Don't run when they politely tell you they don't want to sell. Compliment the area and let them tell you about their neighbors: they may be great sources of information. They may tell you the gossip of the street, which may include someone whose job was recently relocated and who needs to sell, that someone is getting a divorce, or even things like government work planned in the area that could increase the home values. Make notes, and then walk to the next house. When someone says he may be thinking of selling, ask him how much he wants and what the square footage of the home is, then pull out your calculator. Multiply the square footage of that home by what homes are selling for per SF, deduct needed repairs, decide what you feel is the discount you want, and make a noncommittal counter offer such as "What would you think about $xxx,xxx?" Even if you are well below what the homeowner wants, he will likely understand that you are just guessing, and still be kind. You never know when you will hit the right person at the right time.

A few tips on door knocking. Appear less threatening by always showing a side view of your body when they look out the peephole or open the door, and then make constant eye contact. Be pleasant and complimentary. To sellers, refer to the property as a "house," but to prospective buyers, refer to property as a "home." Try not to let the seller talk about the good times watching the kids grow up, because he will start adding the emotional value to your price. You want to take emotion out of the seller and put it into the buyer.

For sale by owner (FISBO)

Most people selling their own property are not offering good deals, but some are. Most FISBOs are by people that have had agents come out and give them estimates on their homes. Either the agent would not take the listing as high as the owner wanted, or the owner calculated the commission the agent would make and figured he could sell at 3% less and both he and the buyer would come out 1.5% ahead on the deal. After all, the going rate of a 6% commission on a $500,000 home is $30,000! But what the FISBOs do not understand is that the exposure of the Multiple Listing Service (MLS) will create greater demand and a higher sale price, not to mention a (hopefully) experienced agent to make sure everything goes down fairly.

Therefore, most FISBOs will have an asking price at or above market value but may be receiving no offers and be willing to drastically drop the price. There are also many FISBOs that have decided how much they want for their property and simply don't want to deal with a middleman in their personal business. Sometimes, a person needs to sell fast for a reduced price and figures that if he reduces the price enough, someone will buy it quickly, but with the reduced price he can't afford to pay an agent's commission. Imagine that homes are selling for $500,000 in the area. The seller knows that the local agents want 6%, and it will cost him $30,000 to sell his home. The most you would ever offer for this house is $470,000, but the FISBO may be willing to take a lot less.

Because of these and a variety of other reasons, FISBOs can be very profitable to hunt down and buy. But be careful: there are some experts out there pretending to be FISBOs! They deceive buyers by trying not to use an escrow company and doing some dirty tricks like transferring the property to someone else moments before your deed is recorded. Always use an escrow company in all transactions and *never* take a recommendation from a FISBO about which escrow company to use!

The easiest way to find a FISBO is in the newspaper advertisements, but remember that the advertising has likely increased the demand. If there is an agent marketing, the word "agent" or some other indication that it is not a FISBO will appear in the ad. For less widely advertised homes, look for the very small local newsletters, which most other homebuyers will overlook. Some social organizations will have newsletters with advertising sections. Yard signs can also be fruitful. If you make regular trips around your target area, you may find a recently posted yard sign that has yet to attract other buyers. Drive down the less beaten path to find those that have less demand because fewer people find them.

Advertising yourself
Many buyers put ads in the paper, signs on trees, or even signs on their cars that say, "We buy houses! Call Me!" If these advertisers were really after a fair price, they would look in the MLS for the home of their

dreams. These people want the desperate FISBOs to come to them so they can make a low offer for a fast and profitable sale. There is nothing wrong with this idea and no reason you can't do the same thing. Put out signs and advertisements, have the sellers call you, find out why they are selling and what they need, do a CMA so you know the value of the house before showing up, make your low offer, and hope they have reasons to take the fast sale. Remember to always find out their needs before making an offer.

The Widow
This method may seem predatory to some, but if you act decently and treat homeowners as human beings, there is no reason it needs to be. There are many older married couples whose children and families have moved to other parts of the country and who chose to stay behind in their homes of thirty years. When one of the couple dies, the surviving spouse may need living assistance and need to move in with a relative immediately. Though people in this situation may have owned their fully paid-off houses for decades, they may not be able to stay and wait for a sale at the full value. They need to liquidate the property fast and move on with their lives. Their children are out of state and have children of their own and no time to help with the move. Remember my story about the elderly couple reduced to living in one room of their mansion, unable to pay their bills though they had the money? When people are stuck in bad situations, deals like this can be advantageous to both parties.

By checking the obituaries in the paper, you can find a list of people who may be in that exact position. Be pleasant and be sympathetic, and if you are visiting, consider a small gift such as a pie or fruit basket. Understand that many people in this situation will dismiss you as a vulture and insult you. Some will invite you in for the company, even though they have no desire to sell their homes. It could take months of rejections to find one person in the right situation, but if your plan is to flip (sell soon after buying), one every few months is all you need. Though you are offering a reduced price, the widow or widower will still be getting more money than he or she paid twenty or thirty years ago. Be mindful of the sellers' needs. Consider assisting with the paperwork, if needed, and perhaps even with the organization and payment of moving trucks. I know brokers that still receive Christmas cards from widows they helped in this way.

If you are planning on flipping, these homes usually require only superficial cosmetic repairs (new carpets and a good paint job) before flipping for a profit. Others require renovation of the kitchens or bathrooms to be more modern. Some jurisdictions require notifying a buyer if a person actually died inside the home for some number of years after the death. This could change your resale profits because it could decrease the demand (people that believe in ghosts won't buy). If someone died on the property, check the laws in your area.

NOD (Notice Of Default)

Novices may refer to these as "pre-foreclosures." After homeowners are delinquent in their loan payments (usually for 3 months), the FI will record with the county recorder a notice of default (NOD). This gives what is called "actual notice" to the homeowner and other relevant parties that the FI is preparing to foreclose on the property if the homeowner cannot pay. You don't need to pay anyone exorbitant fees to learn which homes have NODs: it is public record. You can go down to the recorder periodically and check yourself, but some counties supply this information on a free website. There are also some reasonably priced companies that do the research for you and gather it on their websites, and the value of your time may make it worthwhile to join one of these services. Be sure they send you fresh listings often.

The midnight infomercials are well aware of this tactic, and if you send the homeowner a letter or show up at their door, you will be in competition with dozens of would-be buyers with their midnight infomercial kits in hand. They all hope to steal the property, usually with programs that will not work.

If, however, your mindset is to figure out how best to solve the problems of the delinquent homeowners, you are more likely find to a way to both help them and make yourself a profit. You will need to talk to the homeowners and find out why they are not paying off their loans. While not having the money is the most obvious, there can be many reasons why people default. You will need to find a solution to the problem. Be the problem solver! If the property is so over-indebted that the only way to cure it is a "short sell" (talked about later), unless you can't bear to part with this house, consider moving on to the next property. Normally, however, the homeowner still has some equity in the property. If the property is worth $400,000 and the debt is $300,000, the homeowner has $100,000 in equity. Sometimes, even when an owner has equity, he may have a credit rating so bad he can't refinance to access his equity. Maybe this is some inherited property the owner doesn't care about or a second home. Maybe the owner has lost his job and needs to downgrade his living standard, and you can help by getting him into a $200,000 home. Maybe he had other expenses or his debt got out of hand. If you can find a way out of the problem, you may find a mutually beneficial arrangement.

Whatever the problem is, the homeowner needs to liquidate his ownership in the property before it gets taken away at great loss to him and his credit. A homeowner may try to put the home up for sale at slightly below the market price, but then it becomes a race to find a buyer before he loses his home. Even if he finds a buyer, if that person falls out of escrow, the owner is back to square one and even closer to losing the house. Maybe he would hand the property over to you at no cost if he could live there for one year to get his life back together (called a lease back). All you would have to do is pay the monthly expenses. Let's look again at the $400,000 home with the $300,000 debt. If you take the home for $30,000 up front and the agreement to let the owner live another year in it, then you sell it for the owner's debt of $300,000, you get 90% LTV financing at 6% interest on a $300,000 loan. All you pay during that year is $1,600 a month for the loan payment. After a year, you've spent $19,200 plus your down payment of $30,000, equaling $49,200 for a home with $100,000 in equity. You came out ahead $50,800 in one year. If you add in the expected 8% appreciation of the property over that year, it will be $32,000 more, making you a total of $82,800. The best part is that as you did this, you gave the seller the best opportunity of his life to recover from the problems he was facing.

Let's go back once again to that $400,000 home with $300,000 debt. It's the same situation, except that in this example, you already own another less expensive property, currently vacant. You offer the defaulting homeowner a land contract or lease option on that smaller house at $20,000 under value. From his point of view, his bad credit will keep him from buying a new home for years. You will place him right into a more affordable property without a credit check or any loan. From your point of view, you gained $100,000 equity on his home by giving him $20,000 in equity on another home. While he makes payments in the hope of one day owning this house, he will basically be paying your loan on the smaller house off for you. You net $80,000, and everyone is happy. Another buyer might have been offering the homeowner more money, but you won the bid because you gave him what he really wanted.

Let's go back to that indebted $400,000 house for a final example. Another way to benefit the distressed homeowner is to offer to buy the property for, in this example, $330,000. This is much less than the $400,000 the seller wants to get, but no one is making an offer any higher, and you can close the deal in 30 days. This will give the seller $30,000 in a fast escrow to make a new life, and, to some extent, protect his credit from getting worse. Once his contingencies are gone in the selling of the property, you will likely bring his past-due amount up to date for him as a value, thus protecting what is left of his credit, which will make him go with your offer rather than someone else's.

The important thing about a NOD is that you must listen to the seller and see if you can find a way to meet his needs at little cost to you.

Auctions
The method of foreclosure can vary greatly based on the area, on whether the instrument securing the debt is a mortgage or trust deed, and on whether legal action must be used in that jurisdiction. This may change which method it is best to use to acquire the property.

After a property has been foreclosed, it is usually sold at auction. The government may also auction off property that had been condemned due to illegal activities or back taxes. Proper notice requires that local papers advertise the property, which allows interested buyers to view it, check the values of comparable sales in the neighborhood (comps) and do CMAs. Then there will be an auction, and the highest bidder that can prove he can buy the property will acquire it. Such homes are often not in the best condition, so discount the cost of repairs when you value such a property. Know the value and know how high you are willing to bid before you enter the auction. I have seen the excitement of the auction lead people to bid far beyond what they intended or what the property could possibly be worth. Unless you are lucky and few show up to bid, the property will likely sell for near the true value. This is far from a deal, especially when you may have to pay in cash (no leverage). The best deals can be found on non-conforming property or property that looks more expensive to fix than it actually is. Get a good and detailed estimate of the repair costs in advance.

When an auction is conducted in a remote area or far away from the subject property, it may be an inside deal between the auction company and an investor who wants to keep the demand low. The companies know that few people investigate properties they need to drive across the county to look at. If you go anyway, the low demand could be to your advantage instead of theirs. Some investors only go to such auctions, in hopes of finding special deals.

Be careful of companies that attempt to look like a government auctions but sell remote and nearly valueless land in swamps and deserts. Just because they say it is a "public notice" does not mean the government placed that notice.

Getting back to the midnight infomercials again, many of them talk about buying a house at auction for $25. This is (very) occasionally possible if the government (probably wrongfully) acquired the house because someone lost his tax bill behind the couch, the house was auctioned in some remote hillbilly area, and only one person showed up to bid and got the house for $25. It may happen, but probably about as often as recent divorcees offer to sell their ex-husbands' sports cars for $100. Don't buy the books and tapes: you now know how it is done.

Real Estate Owned (REO)

A FI may acquire a property because of foreclosure on a mortgage, because the original owner forfeited the property (gave it to the FI), or because no one bid the "reserve" (the minimum allowable bid, equal to the amount owed on the loan debt). Contrary to popular belief, FIs don't want to own properties. They try to get rid of them by auction, but when no one bids the minimum required, the FI is stuck with the property. The FI may have to make repairs and be required to put money in a reserve for each home it owns, pay people in the office to oversee the REO department, and compensate local brokers. At the end of all that, the FI may end up selling at a loss. The property is dead weight on which the FI can't make money, and which the FI is responsible for managing, insuring, and protecting, no matter how inconvenient the property location or how much time and manpower it wastes. As you may imagine, the stockholders of the FI are not happy when the FI has too many properties.

The FI wants to dispose of REOs as fast as it can, but it is torn between disposing of properties at a loss before it loses more and trying to recover the losses. Sometimes the FI will deal with a local agent or may have its own department to deal with the sale of these properties. If a property goes through an agent, it is much like any other home for sale but priced slightly below market value to move it quick. Remember that it will be on the Multiple Listing Service (MLS) and seen by all the agents and their clients. If you keep a close watch, however, you may be fast enough to buy this property below value. The much better deal occurs when the FI sells the property directly, trying to recoup its original investment on the loan. By checking the recorder's records or having the title company give you copies, you can find out the debt on the property. If you offer slightly more than that amount to cover the FI's costs, it will likely be cooperative in moving the property. If demand is low and the FI knows it will never get the investment back, it may take an offer under value just to get rid of the property. The FI's desire to get the property out of its name and into yours also means you have a good chance of negotiating a very attractive loan.

Making It Work

We have laid out the framework for how to find areas and types of property to buy. Of course, if you have the cash value of the house sitting in your safe, then you are fine from here on. But most people don't have that kind of money, and even if they did, they would want to leverage the deal to get the most buying power for the money. Besides, you can make good money based on how the deal is organized. Remember the earlier section "The Value of Future Money, Today," when we talked about Wimpy's hamburger? We come back to that concept now as we try to make a reasonable offer to the property owner while giving little or nothing of our own money. We will go over deals where the property owner receives what he wants or needs and the profit is still there for us. Afterwards, we will talk about qualifying for loans, and how you can improve your chances for a good loan in advance. This is not only helpful in itself, but also for the deal: the seller is more likely to accept a lower offer if he knows you can fulfill your side of the bargain.

8. Types of Deals

We will now talk about how to make your deal work and discuss the different types of deals out there. We will also go into what to do with the property once you have it because that goes hand in hand with the type of deal you want to make. You can mix and match the ideas in this book when you apply them to the real world. For instance, you may find a FISBO, do a short sell, and then do room additions. In spite of what the midnight infomercials claim, there is no one plan that works for all properties: all land is unique, as is each person who sells it. You may find two homes next door to each other with the same floor plan, but which you need to acquire by different types of deals and which may be most profitable used in different ways. My aim in this book is to give you the building blocks, which you can recombine in the way that suits you and your prospective property best.

Although the concepts of real estate have stayed the same for a thousand years, and the major laws have changed little in the last hundred, the laws do change. The rules of real estate vary from area to area, and FIs can change their procedures with little notice. I will tell you about theories that have been used for decades and laws that apply almost everywhere, but some of the "tricks" I describe may not be legal in your area, or perhaps anywhere. People in the industry use these tricks, and it is important that you understand and be able to recognize them, especially if someone tries to use them against you. Always double-check the laws in your area, and remember that I have included here for completeness's sake many things I do not recommend.

Short sell
Sometimes a FI is so dissatisfied with its investment in the loan on a property that it would rather lose money than deal with the current owner or foreclose. There can be many reasons for this. Maybe the unemployed current owner has been constantly late in payments. Maybe the property has devalued so much that even selling would not recoup the loss. Maybe the type of use of the property will attract few buyers at auction, and it is unlikely the FI can recover its expenses (for example, an

apartment building in a high-vacancy area). In certain cases, the FI would rather offer a financially secure owner a reduced loan amount than deal with the property as a REO.

Consider first approaching the homeowner in the way we described in the section "Finding the Right Seller" to see whether you can find a solution to the problem. If the property is in enough debt that the answer is a short sell, and you decide that the property is still worth your while, get the short sell package from the FI and have the homeowners spell out their financial problems on paper. Contact the FI and fill out the required documentation so that you can make a deal with the FI to reduce the loan amount when it transfers the property to a new buyer.

You can find these properties either through the Notice of Defaults (NOD) lists or by checking the local real estate listings for properties that have been listed for a long time and had several decreases in asking price. When you go door to door and find an owner who tells you he would like to sell but can't because he would lose money, a short sell is the answer. Like all things with real estate, it sounds complicated, but all you have to do is follow the instruction book the FI will give you. Once you, the FI, and the owner have agreed on a deal, experts will take care of the rest.

A short sell is not the seller's first choice, but if he has no equity and will lose the house anyway, he is better off walking away with his credit rating relatively undamaged. Some investors claim in advertisements that a short sell is beneficial to homeowners with equity, but it is rarely the best option. Perhaps if a seller were to lie to the FI about not making enough money, find an appraiser to lie about the house value, fail to tell the FI that the buyer is his sister-in-law, and secretly receive a cut of the profit she stole from the FI, then it could be profitable. This, however, is fraud, and that extra profit will not seem so great from jail.

You hear a lot about short sells that happen (or seem to happen), but you tend to hear little about the downside of waiting for the FI to agree to the deal. I recall one buyer who said he had been in three failed short sell deals that tied up his time and money, and that he would never try one again. There can be good profit in a short sell, but this is not for the buyer who wants a quick close.

Lease option to sublease

In a typical lease option (like the one we talked about with William) you lease the property, paying a little more than the normal rent for the right to buy the property in the future for a fixed amount of money. Locking in the price at today's value can be beneficial for a person who does not yet have the funds to buy the house. However, there is a much more innovative way for the forward-thinking entrepreneur to use this to his benefit. Let's say you get a lease option with right to sublease, where you can buy the property for $400,000 (the current value) for the next five or ten years. You are responsible for the rent being paid to the owner, but you can sublease the property to someone else. If you negotiate well, you can get your cost to lease and the tenant's cost to sublease to be about the same. Even if you lose a little each month from the difference, the end result will be a great return on your investment. Adjusting for some vacancy problems over time, you could have several of these going simultaneously. You become the landlord's middleman. Right before the option expires five or ten years later, you then exercise your option! You are using yesterday's price to buy today's property. The property has inflated in price by about 8% per year to a current value of $587,750, but you can buy it at $400,000. Almost any FI will loan you money for this deal, even if you have little or no cash yourself. You could also resell the option or, in what is called a double escrow, sell the property instantaneously to someone else and reap the profit without ever spending any of your own money. In other words, you spend some time today (but no money!) working out the deal, make sure you have a tenant in the house for the next few years, and in 4 years you will have made $187,750.

Let's see how this would work if you had several of these deals. Let's say you set up five of these subleased lease options on $400,000 properties, each with an option period of five years. By the end of five years, the properties have increased 50% in value (8.45 appreciation per year), so that each is worth $600,000. When you buy the property, you make $200,000 X 5 = $1,000,000 in 5 years, using little or none of your own money! Now let's make the deal a little worse and say that you couldn't get the tenant to pay quite as much as you did, and lost an average of $200 on each of those five homes per month for those five years. You would have slowly invested $60,000 over those years, but you would still have $1,000,000 at the end. And even in that scenario, after the first two years, you should have been able to increase the rent to make up for short-term loss. Before the fourth year, you could actually be making a little money on rent while you watch your investments grow.

Shared equity

In shared equity, two people buy one piece of property under a very stringent contract. One person finds the property, comes up with a down payment, and has the needed credit. The other person lives on the property and pays all the loan, tax, and upkeep expenses. Eventually, they sell the house and split the profit. I know that some midnight infomercials market this as a nothing down deal, but this only happens if you get a reduction in price from the original owner and then deceive your new partner about the cost and make him pay the down payment. We will instead assume a fair deal.

While the usefulness of this arrangement has its limits (as we will discuss below), there are situations where this deal can meet both partners' particular needs. One partner has credit and extra money, while the other has a limited income and wants to be a homeowner. This can work if the financially stable person has a responsible adult child or relative that cannot qualify for a home unaided but who wants to build credit and reap the benefits of home ownership.

I don't recommend getting into shared equity partnerships, even with trusted partners and full disclosure of all the facts. There is simply too much that can go wrong when you count on someone else to hold up his side of a deal, especially when the two of you may have to make future decisions unanimously. Think ahead to when your partner is not keeping the yard clean and you need to fight with him about differing conceptions of yard work. If the partners are less cooperative, worse situations can arise. The home is usually in the name of the partner that supplied the down payment, giving him control. The person on the title can use any of several reasons to kick the other partner off the deal so that the latter has paid the loan and upkeep on a home from which he will receive nothing.

Frankly, anyone with the money and credit to be the buying partner in a shared equity would be better off buying and then renting out the property. Anyone in a situation such that they would want to be the tenant partner would probably be better off finding a lease option deal. The only profitable reason I can think of for a title-holder to have a shared equity partner is to force the latter to pay taxes, loan, and upkeep, and then kick him out of the deal. To put it simply: consider very carefully before you agree to be someone's equity partner.

If, however, you are a parent who wants to do your adult child a great favor while keeping control to make sure your child fulfills his duties, this can be helpful.

Double escrow
A double escrow occurs when the new buyer resells the property before ever taking title to the property. This is a common no-money-down type of deal that can be used no matter how bad your credit is at the time. The idea is really rather easy! First, we have to start with an undervalued piece of property that we found using one of the methods we discussed previously. When you make the deal, you make sure your contract with the original sellers allows you some contingencies to get out of the deal and a right to assign the contract ("buyer to be John Doe and/or assignee"). Contingencies are ways that you can change your mind about whether you want to buy the property so there will be no cost to you for backing out. The right to inspect the property, for instance, can be a contingency. In the purchase contract, you give yourself as much time to back out as possible and also ask for the longest escrow you can negotiate. Most sophisticated sellers will not allow you to have such a simple way out for more than 10 to 15 days, but I don't believe any state has a law forbidding these contingencies from lasting the full length of the escrow period, generally about three months. In the contract, you stipulate that you have the right to view the home as often as you wish and that you can bring others to view the home with you.

At the same time, or even before you found the house to buy, you advertise and find a person that wants to buy a home. Or maybe you don't have a potential buyer waiting beforehand, but you advertise the property after you have a contract with the original sellers. You then take your potential buyers with you to view the home you are under contract to buy. It is best not to tell the original owners that you are bringing potential buyers. You then sell the property you do not yet own to your potential buyers for more money than you will be paying the original sellers. Escrow will run its course, and at the moment escrow closes, the property will transfer to you for a moment, then transfer to the buyers you have found. Or, if you were able to get the assignment clause in the purchase contract, you simply hand over the deal to the new buyer, for a price. The difference in money between what you purchased the property for and what your buyers are paying will go to you. You have just made a good chunk of money with no money down and none of your credit used, in which everyone received what he wanted.

Here is an example: you find a property worth $400,000. The owner will let you buy it for $350,000. You price it for a fast sale at $380,000. You made $30,000 in the one second that you owned the property.

Long-term Option
This is best used to buy raw land, but it can also be used for other types of property. First, as always, you need to find the property you plan on using. With this plan, it is best to use an assessor's records to find raw land (land that has nothing built on it) that has been held for a long time by the same person or a person that has an out-of-state address. The assessor's list shows the date the owner acquired the property, so it is easy to make a good contact list. Many people bought land long ago or inherited property they have almost forgotten they own. Second, as always, you find the going value for the property by checking recent sales in the area. Then, you contact the owner and, instead of just offering to buy the property, you offer them an "option." What this means is that you give them a small amount of money to hold the property for you to buy sometime in the future for a fixed amount of money. Example: "I will give you [$100] now for the right for [myself], or assignee, to buy [your land] anytime in the next [5] years for [$40,000]."

Although some sellers may require more than $100 for an option to buy their property, many will be willing to settle. People who have owned land for a long time usually are not in a hurry to sell it and don't mind making something small and perhaps have the property sold soon without having to spend the time, trouble, or money.

You now have a power in that land. All you have to do is find someone willing to buy it within the option period for more than what you can buy it for. Since it is raw land, it is easy for your potential buyers to examine it. Land takes time to sell, so you could spend three years waiting with your sign on the land. But after all, you only have $100 invested. Once you have found a buyer, you simply transfer the option to him as an assignee for whatever he is willing to pay over the option price. Your potential buyer actually buys your option from you and then uses your option to buy the property. You never ended up owning the land, and the worst-case risk you were facing was not finding a buyer to sell the option to and losing the $100 you gave to the original sellers.

I knew of an investor who made long-term option contracts all the time. He never searched for anyone to buy the property and spent all his time buying more options near areas where local development would soon create demand. He figured that if he had about fifty lots, eventually people would come to him, which they did. Sometimes a buyer would contact the seller directly, and he would split the profit with the seller to get out of the option.

Buying and foreclosing on second deeds
The popular belief about how this works is not true. People believe that they can sell homeowners second mortgages and when the homeowners default, the properties go to the lenders. Example: Homeowner has a $500,000 home and a debt to FI for $100,000, but can't pay his bills. Investor loans Homeowner $10,000, knowing Homeowner can't pay it back. When Homeowner defaults, Investor kicks out Homeowner and owns the $500,000 home. Investor sells the home, pays off the FI's $100,000, and keeps the $400,000 with only a $10,000 investment. Not true! Some investors think they never even have to pay off the FI. In reality, if a home gets auctioned, the homeowner gets whatever money is left over!

As a real estate attorney, I have had many people come to me claiming their homes were stolen this way and wanting me to recover their property. With some minor investigations, I always find that the home was over-indebted and the owner received many legal notices, which he threw away. Then there was a legal auction at which the home sold for less than the homeowner had in debt. Unfortunately for heavily indebted homeowners, the big companies are normally very careful in following the requirements. Only on very rare occasions have I read in the real estate journals of a small company that deliberately defrauded people by not giving notices, holding unadvertised auctions, or misappropriating the extra money. Most of the stories you hear about unfairly repossessed houses come from the delinquent homeowners failing to take responsibility for their excessive debt or to deal with the FIs before the debt snowballed with legally added fees. The odds are that the homeowner received little or no money because there was little or no equity left in the home.

Another reason people think this can be done is because some midnight infomercials give the impression that people are taking homes for the cost of a small second mortgage. After a person buys that $500 midnight infomercial kit, he will find that the infomercial was describing discounting notes, which we will talk about next.

Buying Seconds at Discount
Although this sounds like a real estate deal and really does involve real estate, it is more like an investment. Just as it would be great to buy a $50,000 stamp collection for $5,000, it would be equally valuable to buy a $50,000 secured debt (meaning the property is collateral—i.e. a mortgage) for $5,000. Here, Homeowner has a $500,000 home with a first mortgage to the FI of $100,000 and a second mortgage of $50,000. The investor contacts the holder (person to whom the debt is owed) and asks him if he will take less money if the investor can pay off the loan in full immediately. The holder of the second mortgage could be in a lot of situations where this might be of value to him: maybe he is a contractor who did some work on the property and doesn't think he will ever be paid back, maybe it is the widow who sold the property to Homeowner and took a carry back loan (loan from the seller to the buyer), or maybe it is another investor who simply needs the money now. If you contact lots of second holders of notes and offer them discounts, some of them will be willing to discount the note of debt in order to be paid something today.

The midnight infomercials talk about this trick, but they tell you to go through county recorder records (or another service with the information) and contact people that have received NODs (Notices of Default), then contact the second deed owners (people who gave a second loan on a house) of the properties to see if you can buy the second mortgage at a discount. The infomercials describe this as a sure profit when the house is foreclosed on, but let's look more closely. Once you hold a homeowner's second mortgage, there are essentially three possible outcomes. The first is that the homeowner pays off his mortgage and keeps his home. The second is that the house is foreclosed on and sells at auction for high enough to pay off the debts. The third is that the house is foreclosed on, but no one bids high enough to pay the debts. In the first case, you will be paid over a period of years, which can be profitable if you can afford to have your money tied up for a long period of time, since you will make good interest. In the second case, your profit is simply the difference between what you bought the mortgage for and what it was worth. In the third case, however, you lose your investment. Before you enter into a deal like this, be certain that you can afford to wait a while for your profit if the homeowner comes through, and be sure that if the house is auctioned, it will sell at a price high enough to pay you.

Here is a realistic example of how this can work. You find someone who has the rights to recover on a debt, in this case let us say a widow in need of cash today, who is a holder of second mortgage note on a property for $50,000 at 6% interest based on a 10 year balloon (meaning the homeowner will pay nothing for 10 years, and then pay it all). The widow has been receiving $0 each month but would rather have $25,000 cash today for her medical bills, so she sells you the note. If the homeowner is foreclosed on and the home sells at auction for enough to repay its debts, or else if the homeowner refinances the property, you get paid the full $50,000, doubling your investment in a short time. However, if the owner makes good on the note, in 10 years it will be worth $89,542, and your rate of return on your $25,000 investment by receiving this note will be 13%. Had the widow accepted your first offer of only $10,000 for that $50,000 note, your rate of return would be 24.5%! If you have extra cash and a good financial calculator, you can make very good money by placing your cash in discounted notes. However, you must make sure that the home will sell at auction for greater than the price of the mortgages on it before you enter into this deal. Make sure there is no subordination clause, which would make it possible for a new note to supplant your second note, turning your note into a third.

There are some great financial calculators that can not only figure out what interest you will receive, but can also discount notes and bonds. I have used the HP12C since the mid 1980s and love it. Some people swear by the Sharp Corporations products. With a small amount of training, these are not hard to use. Understand that because they don't calculate small variables such as how many days are in each month, they will be a few dollars off. They are, however, close enough to determine how good a deal is. Escrow will use a bigger, better program that will work it out to the penny.

If you own a financial calculator, a good advanced tip for getting closer to an accurate value is to avoid using the program's option to divide the interest rate by 12 to get the monthly interest. This tends to mis-estimate the compounding of monthly interest. Per my calculator, $100.00 at 12% interest is 1% per month, and in one year the person would owe me $112.68. This is wrong because 12% interest on $100.00 should be $112.00; we added 68 cents. You are better off first calculating the true monthly interest rate. First, use figures you know and do the math backwards to find the right amount to enter for the interest function. We know that 12% interest per year on $100.00 would be $112.00 in 12 months. We enter those numbers and let the calculator determine that the true interest per month is .9489% per month. Now we have the real monthly interest figure to use for any monthly calculation of 12%.

Because a note holder has a stake in the property, you can buy a discounted note in conjunction with other methods of acquiring property. Example: The NOD homeowner owns a $500,000 home with a $300,000 first mortgage to a private lender and a second to the widow for $50,000 and therefore has $150,000 equity in the property. However, his bad credit will not allow him to access that money, and he can't afford the payments. You offer the widow $100 for a 3 month option to buy the $50,000 note for $25,000. You then go to the NOD homeowner and explain the tax consequences and credit difficulties a foreclosure will cause him. You inform the homeowner that if he will sign over his property to you, you will give him $50,000 in cash. You explain to the private lender how expensive the coming foreclosure will be for him, and offer to buy the $300,000 note for $200,000. You take over the $500,000 property and get an 80% loan of $400,000. The escrow will pay off the notes on the property, which will be $300,000 on the first and $50,000 on the second. Since you now own both, this money goes to you directly. You pay the widow $25,000, the private lender $200,000 and the seller $50,000. You end up owning a $500,000 home with a $400,000 debt and $74,900 in your pocket.

Buy and Lease Back/Option
This could be the deal of a lifetime for the defaulting homeowner and a good profit for you as well. Let's say the homeowner is having financial difficulties but is foreseeing some big money down the line because of a law suit, insurance proceeds, inheritance, because his business is about to take off, etc. Assume his home is valued at $500,000 and he owes the FI $350,000. He therefore has $150,000 in equity, but doesn't want to sell the home. You offer to buy his home for $400,000 and lease it back to him for two years at the cost of your payments (based on a $400,000 loan, taxes, and repairs of the house), with an option allowing him to buy

the house within those two years for $450,000.

Here is how this would work. From the homeowner's point of view, it is better than losing the home, and he gets $50,000 cash now to get him out of whatever trouble he has. He can still live in the house as long as he keeps making payments, and if he straightens out his life, he can buy it back. From your point of view, you have nothing down and 100% financing on a home based on your good credit, with no costs or fees for two years. Either the homeowner pays you back and you make $50,000, or the homeowner loses the house and you sell the property for $500,000 plus appreciation.

If you do this deal honestly, you have bought the home for less because the homeowner was going to lose it anyway, and you get a built-in tenant. If the homeowner can pay you fair market value for it, he gets it back and is better off than he would have been if you hadn't stepped in.

I have heard of some dishonest people who want to get around the "usury laws" (it is against the law to charge ridiculously high interest) by pretending to buy the above homeowner's property but instead doing a *lease back* (the seller leases the home from the buyer) to force him to overpay on interest. Here is a dishonest and probably illegal example: Homeowner needs a quick $40,000 for 6 months, so Investor buys the house for $40,000 over the mortgage debt, giving Homeowner $40,000 cash. Investor gives Homeowner an option to buy back the house in 6 months for $80,000 over mortgage debt. What the Investor really did was charge 100% interest for half a year! Be careful in wording your contract. Make sure it says you bought the home at a bargain intending to keep it and will sell it for a fair price.

9. Fixer-uppers

We are going to need to go into a little more depth here, because how you pick your property and what you do with it will make or break your profit. When examining a fixer-upper to buy, it's easy to misevaluate the required repairs and their costs. Often, what is being marketed as a "fixer-upper" is actually priced at the market value if it were fixed, minus the cost to fix it. Example: a $400,000 home is being sold at $380,000 because it needs a new $20,000 roof. Remember that you are also buying the work and discomfort of fixing the home, and that merits a discount. When you have finished the above house, you will have spent as much as you would pay for a similar home already repaired. Your losses are worse than inconvenience: you have come out behind because you had a hard time getting a loan on a house with a bad roof, and you had to pay for the repairs in cash. Either you lived in the house with carpenters walking around, or you left the property vacant and unproductive as you faced building delays. Maybe if you were a roofing contractor, you could see a value in this—except that whatever time you spend on the house would have been more profitable if someone else had bought the house and hired you to fix it.

Depending on the area and market conditions, you want at least 10% profit minimum for dealing with a fixer-upper. Price + needed repairs x 110 should equal less than current market value. For example, you find that homes in good condition of equal size are selling in the area for $500,000. You find a fixer-upper for $425,000 that will cost you $25,000 to bring up to the same level as the other homes. Your cost going in is $450,000. The value of investing your money in this house and paying cash to fix it is worth 10% of the house, so add 10% ($45,000), and we come to $495,000. As it is less than the area market value, this deal is decent, but not great.

Once you have properly evaluated and picked out your house, it is time to choose which repairs will net you the highest profit. It is important that you make the improvements to meet the needs of the unknown person who will eventually buy the property from you. It would not be a good return on your money to build a lavish disco entertainer's backyard in a neighborhood where the buyers are low-income senior citizens.

Some improvements have different rates of return from area to area. Perhaps the best example is that installing a relatively cheap $1,000 fireplace in the master bedroom will increase the demand for a home because people are willing to pay $4,000 more for the emotional warmth value. On the other hand, a very expensive $20,000 small pool will limit the demand because there are people who don't want the hassle of taking care of a pool. You will probably only increase the value by about $15,000, losing 25% of your investment building the pool.

The easiest and usually most accurate method of estimating the value of a property is by square footage (SF), but SF isn't everything. Two houses with equal square footage next door to each other may use the space in very different ways, leading to differences in demand. Maybe one has three bedrooms and two bathrooms, but the other has five very small bedrooms and only one bathroom. Both homes may be worth the same on paper, but more middle-class buyers will want to see the three-bedroom home, so it is more likely to sell for what it is worth. With few buyers viewing the five-bedroom, the seller will need to reduce the price to motivate more people to look at the property. However, in a low-income area, people may pay more for five smaller rooms they can rent out to friends to help make their payments.

Remember when we talked about how neighborhoods have life cycles of their own? This will play a big part in how you pick the right property, based on your intentions and the amount of repair you are willing to do. If the neighborhood is in decline, subdividing a house for greater rent value may be the most profitable. If the property has hit bottom and is recovering, then maybe only cosmetic attention is needed for a fast sale (a "flip"). If the property is nearing its crest of highest and best use, additional square footage may bring the highest profit. You need to evaluate the neighborhood's present condition so you can predict the needs of future buyers.

Cosmetic Repairs
Sometimes cleaning, painting, and other non-construction adjustments are all it takes to beautify a home up to the quality of the neighborhood. Sometimes all a home needs to get demand from buyers is the "curb appeal" (how it looks from the curb) it would get from some lively front-

yard plants. As I warned previously, watch out for homes that are discounted only by the amount it would cost to make these repairs. Most homes that you can buy at a discount will require some cosmetic repairs because the original owners likely did not care for them and may have taken everything down to the doorknobs when they left.

A good real estate agent will tell the prospective seller that a few dollars to touch up the paint or add some plants will increase demand. Sometimes the agent will talk the seller into more costly repairs to get the best price for the home. Some sellers who are old, low on funds, or outright stubborn will make no cosmetic repairs. The average buyer driving by an unpainted, unbeautified house may be unwilling even to go in to look, so the owner needs to drop the price to sell. This can be an opportunity: I have seen many homes purchased for low prices that needed only very inexpensive cosmetic repairs to be resold at the going price for the area.

I was once called in by a seller to deal with his $400,000 house where the tenant of over 10 years wanted to buy the house but thought he had the right to reduce his offer to only $300,000, $100,000 of which the seller would carry back (loan to the buyer) for 10 years at 0% interest with no monthly payments, and the seller would pay half the buyer's interest on his $200,000 FI loan for 30 years. Without doing the math, I can tell you that the owner would have been better off giving the tenant the property outright than accepting this offer. In order to force the seller to accept this ridiculous offer, the tenant refused to let any buyers view the home. I went by to see if I could politely work out an innovative way for the tenants to buy the property or else have the owner pay them to move. Before I could inform them of my offer to give them $10,000 to move, they called the police on me. After I evicted them, I found they had taken with them the doors, rugs, and toilets. Frankly, all those cosmetic repairs cost less than the $10,000 I would have offered them to be reasonable and leave voluntarily.

A common error people make is to try to save money by cutting corners on cosmetic repairs. If the carpet needs to be replaced, the inexperienced renovator replaces it with the cheapest-grade bright green carpet he can find from a remnant sale. Assuming this house is in a decent area of town, potential buyers will look at the home with the cost of replacing the cheap carpet in mind, reducing demand and the possibility the seller will get the price he anticipates. Do your repairs with the unknown buyer's tastes in mind. This isn't as hard as it sounds. Look at the neighborhood and see what classes of people are moving in and where they are in their lives. A neighborhood that is attracting the elderly will have very different tastes than ones attracting young business people or families. If the neighborhood is diversified or you're unsure, keep cosmetic repairs as middle-of-the-road as you can so you'll have as many prospective buyers as possible and increase demand. Walk into the local paint store and ask which is the most popular off-white paint: now you know what color paint to use inside to be the most palatable to the most buyers.

The buyer should not see anything overly eye-catching that he would find unlivable and have to tear out. Sure, burgundy walls in the kitchen can make a home artistic to young professionals, but that only works if only artsy young professionals are attracted to the neighborhood. Most buyers will be thinking about how many coats of paint it will take to hide the color, and how all that stinky painting will have to be done before they move in. The fewer interested buyers you attract, the less likely you are to get top value. It comes down to supply and demand, and the more demand you can get by decorating for the middle of the market, the more you can sell for.

Renovations
The line between cosmetic repairs and renovations can be blurry. For example, putting a new tile floor in a bathroom could be classified as either one. A good way to think about it is that a renovation is normally more costly and extensive than cosmetic repair. Maybe the home was built in the 1960s and has such an outdated kitchen that the kitchen needs to be torn out and replaced. Maybe some inside walls need to be moved to enlarge the master bedroom. Maybe the front of the home has a shape that is unattractive by today's standards and needs an overhaul. The above examples would be renovations. Unlike cosmetic repairs, where the home is simply being beautified, in a renovation the home is being modernized to the new highest and best use for the current demands of the area.

Even if your intention is to live for many years in the home, whenever you make improvements, you should still take into consideration what value you are adding to the property and what increased demand you can create. Eventually you will sell the home, and you will want to recoup your costs for improvements. Or else, maybe when you refinance you will want the home to appraise as high as possible. I have twice seen cat lovers who decided to make their homes wonderful for their cats. They built special walkways and perches overhead that allowed their cats to walk from room to room through the walls. These very cute "catwalks" make the cats happy, but appraisers have no way to assign them value, and the buyers are limited to cat lovers who don't mind having a house that is better set up for cats than people. In this example, if a thousand prospective buyers looked at the house, 999 would have been thinking of the cost to take out the catwalks for every one that actually wanted them. That one would see that no one else was making offers, so even he, the ideal target of the housing improvements, could lower his offer to match demand.

We have used the term "highest and best use" several times. Let's define the term more carefully before we go on. Highest and best use means that, based on the area and the needs of the people, the current use of the property attracts more buyers than any other use. The highest and best use of land next to an airport may be a parking lot, hotel, or gas station. A senior living center, prison, or school on that property would have much lower demand. Whenever you make renovations to a property, consider the highest and best use.

Maybe you find a home in a neighborhood that the elderly are moving into, but you notice that most of the other homes have steps leading to the front door: perhaps a handicap ramp would increase the demand for your property. Maybe you find a home built in the 1940s, and the rooms are closed-off and dark. Opening walls and adding skylights would increase demand. Maybe a home has a view but nowhere to stand and look at it. Adding a raised entertainer's deck would have buyers marveling at the sunset and forgetting about the small rooms the house has to offer. I could go on for a week talking about the "maybe this or that," because the options you will have are limitless.

Before you buy a property, drive around the neighborhood. Check the demographics of who is living there and who is buying homes. Go to open houses on the weekends and find out which homes suit the area and which ones don't. Figure out what makes a home less than the going price and what would bring it up to the average. In more diverse neighborhoods, consider what would be the best use of this home by the likely buyers and how best to adjust the home to that demand. Determine what those improvements will add to the value of the property first, then find out the cost of making them.

I have seen people first find out the cost of an improvement they really want and then try to justify it in terms of far-fetched profits and unlikely demand. One such misguided client of mine wanted to build an auto body shop in his large back yard, explaining that some buyer might want to make extra cash fixing the neighbor's cars. I could not convince him that it was more likely that his middle-class neighbors would be calling the city concerning his zoning violations. A renovation can be costly, and you will want to make sure it does something for you besides take up your money and time. Sit down and do the math before you start.

Subdividing
Subdividing usually means dividing a large section of land to be desirable to people who would rather pay more per square foot for smaller parcels of raw land. We talked about this previously in the examples of farmland being bought up and separated into smaller parcels for homes. Here we will talk instead about dividing a large home into small rental units. Some people buy homes slightly larger than their families need in anticipation of some tenant paying a good part of the loan payments. Even in Beverly Hills people are dividing up homes for multiple tenants for a lower cost per person. You may not want to turn a property into an apartment building, but there may be a home with room to make a one-bedroom rental that might be more profitable as two bachelor apartments.

Changing a large house into multiple rental units can bring profit whether you keep the property or sell it. We talked about the law of diminishing returns above: let's use that theory. Remember that return on investment is greater as you bring the property up to the standard of the neighborhood and that it becomes less as you overbuild. The same concept works on renting property. Assume that a 400 SF single room apartment costs $400. For only $100 more, you can get a one-bedroom at 600 SF. For another $50, you can get a two-bedroom at 800 SF.

Compare the cost per SF of these situations:

Bachelors	400 SF @ $400	= $1.00 per square foot
One bedroom	600 SF @ $500	= $0.83 per square foot
Two Bedrooms	800 SF @ $550	= $0.67 per square foot

From a renter's point of view, by paying just a little more, you can get a better value for the amount of property you live in. But we are landowners now, so we reverse the idea. The smaller the space we rent out, the more the tenants pay per square foot.

Say that we as landlords have purchased a large four-bedroom home, zoned to be multi-residential in what used to be a high-class neighborhood but which has been declining towards rentals. Let's say the going price for a four-bedroom, 2,200 SF home is $400,000, and at 80% Loan to Value (LTV) our monthly loan debt is around $2,400. Now let's say the monthly cost of property taxes and insurance is $300, making our monthly cost to keep this property $2,700. Families are renting similar homes at $3,000 per month, so if we do so, we make $300 per month and reap all the benefits of homeownership and the appreciated value when we sell. It's not a bad return, but let's see whether putting in some bedroom door locks will increase our profit.

We find that the demand for single boarding rooms in homes is very high and there is little supply, so people will pay $1,000 per month to have a room and share a kitchen and bathrooms. We could rent each room out separately and make $4,000 per month in income. After the onetime cost of putting new locks on a few doors and paying our $2,700 monthly costs, we profit $1,300 per month.

As you can see, we make $1,000 more per month by subdividing the property into bedrooms with shared bathrooms and kitchen. Even if we had to pay $24,000 to legally divide the home into a 4-plex, we make that investment back in two years and make an extra $12,000 a year in profit over the un-subdivided option. Because, our return on investment of the $24,000 cost of building is paid back in 2 years, when four years have passed, we will have doubled our profit. Now, instead of profiting as landlords ourselves, let's look at quickly selling the now legal 4-plex to a buyer. Remember earlier when we talked about the income approach to evaluating property? An investment buyer will calculate the income of the fully rented house and may pay $80,000 over what someone would pay merely to live in it.

As you can see in this example, we have made a profit in only a few months of work. If you are considering this, remember there may be local codes to meet, which you should verify before closing escrow on the house. You can put in your offer a contingency that gives you a week or two to check this out and still get out of the deal if you see problems. During that time, you can have contractors bid on your proposed changes. After you buy and subdivide the house, make sure you get it fully rented with leases as long as possible before putting it back on the market as an income investment.

Additions

Adding square footage can make the most profit, if you do it right. Do not get into this unless you have some money to back you and some knowledge of construction. In order to understand how to pick a likely home for this purpose, we again go back to the law of diminishing returns. The average neighborhood will have homes that are largely similar to each other. Let's say in our neighborhood that all the homes are about the same age, two or three bedrooms, and approximately 1,800 SF. If we value them with the Market Approach, the value will be the average per-SF selling price of the area, multiplied by the SF of the subject home. Let's do an example in a high-priced neighborhood:

Comparables (comps) assuming Home Y is average for the neighborhood:
Home X is 1,400 SF and sold for $630,000, thus $450 per SF
Home Y is 1,800 SF and sold for $792,000, thus $440 per SF
Home Z is 2,200 SF and sold for $902,000, thus $410 per SF

Looking at these numbers, you can see that for the smaller Home X, people will pay more per square foot (SF) to live in the neighborhood of nicer and bigger homes. The people that purchased the biggest Home Z have the least value per SF because they are nestled with smaller homes. If Home Z were to put a second floor on it to raise its SF to 4,400, no one would pay $1,804,000 to live in a home surrounded by homes of one third the value. Therefore, the price per SF increases most when a home under the neighborhood average is renovated to be only slightly larger than the average.

A client of mine once wanted to know why no bank would refinance his brand-new home. He had purchased a vacant lot in a depressed area of tiny, single-story homes, put up a big wall around the outside, and built a marble-lined two-story mansion on every inch of available land. The client said his property was several times the size of the other homes, and much better built. I had to tell him that his home was only worth what someone would pay for it, and the demand to live in that part of town was only from people who could not afford anything else. I also pointed out that most people that could pay for a house that size would want some backyard, and his did not have one. In other words, don't oversize and don't build something too dissimilar to your area.

Let's look more closely at the examples above. Say we buy Home X at list price. Assume the going price to build in the area is $100 per SF and we decide to increase the home by adding an extra 400 SF bedroom to bring the size up to that of Home Y. We pay the contractor $100 X 400 SF, $40,000. We pay our purchase price of $630,000 and our construction price of $40,000, and let's even add in $6,000 lost income for the four months the property is vacant for construction, for a total investment of $676,000. The home will be the same value as Home Y, $792,000, and will bring us a net profit of $116,000. If we had gotten a discount on the house, were living in the home at the time, or had done some of the work ourselves, the profit would be much higher.

To make this clear, let's add 400 SF to each home and see how we come out.

X becomes 1,800 SF x value $440 SF = $792,000, increase of $162,000
Y becomes 2,200 SF x value $410 SF = $902,000, increase of $110,000
Z becomes 2,600 SF x value $370 SF = $962,000, increase of $60,000

In our Home Z, the one already oversized, we spend $40,000 to build and $6,000 for vacancy factors, increase the price by $60,000, and make barely any money ($14,000) after costs. Beware of overbuilding!

Now we can take this idea one step further. Let's say we find Home Q, which is 1,400 SF (the same size as Home X) but needs cosmetic repairs and minor construction because it has been neglected. The original owner has discounted the home $30,000 because it needs $25,000 to bring it up to current standards with the neighborhood (new kitchen, upgraded baths, and carpets). We buy the home for a fair price of $600,000. However, it will not cost us the full $25,000 to fix it because we are already planning construction on the property. Part or all of the money we were going to spend on the addition may overlap with the cost of refurbishing. One of the cosmetic repairs may have been painting the exterior of the home, but if we're building an addition, we have to repaint anyway. The four-month vacancy of the property also overlaps, so we only need to count it in our costs once. It could even be that the part of the house we expand removes part of the house that needed repairs. Using the law of diminishing returns once again, the more work the contractor does, the better the price he is likely to give us. So instead of $40,000 for the addition and $25,000 for the cosmetic, he bids you $55,000 for the full job. We have increased our profit by at least another $10,000!

The construction cost in the example above was $100 per SF, but that cost is rarely a flat rate and depends on a variety of factors. Are the walls brick or wood? Is the foundation raised or slab? Are we putting in carpet or marble? Are we using already-existing walls to save on building costs? Another major factor is *what* is being built. The square feet where electrical wiring or water is being added will cost a lot more than the empty space in a room. A nice 40 SF bathroom could cost more than a 400 SF bedroom. And with the different building codes and the cost of labor, the price varies dramatically across the country.

Your job is to think about the best improvements for the lowest cost. If the main problem with the home is that it only has one bathroom, then adding a second may be almost mandatory. But avoid expensive per-SF costs if you can. Even if you do have to build that new bathroom, try to build it near the kitchen or other bathroom to keep from having to run the plumbing far.

One of the most profitable additions can be converting a garage into a bedroom. Many cities allow this, though some require an inexpensive carport or other form of off-street parking to replace the garage. Since the old garage was not calculated in the price paid per living SF and already had walls and a roof, it is cheaper to add SF by insulating it and putting up drywall than by building a room in the backyard. The demand will drop slightly to those that are willing to have only a carport for their cars, but the greater square footage will raise the home value enough to compensate.

10. Credit

Almost every real estate deal involves a loan, and paying that loan will be a major expense. Since the lower your expenses are, the more you make, saving on that loan is very important. Without good credit, you will either not be able to get a loan, or you will pay too much on any loan you get. Therefore, you will need to look at your credit in advance to set yourself up for the best lending bargains.

The attorney comes out in me when I start writing about credit and loans. I have some strong moral opinions that some in the industry may not appreciate. My office was trying to sell reasonable loans to people back in 2005 when our competition was selling negative amortization balloon payment sub-prime loans to people they knew would lose the homes. It would be impossible for me to give a proper overview of real estate without discussing some of the more questionable tactics that some people in the business use. A few of the things I will talk about may be on the borderline of ethical. Others may be fraud or otherwise illegal in some or all jurisdictions. The FIs base their interest rates on formulas that evaluate the risk posed by each client. It is illegal to deceive a FI into making loans at terms it would otherwise not make. Do I believe that these deceptions happen by the thousands each day? YES! That does not mean I condone or advise anyone to use unethical methods. My intention is to warn you about some of the pitfalls that can go unnoticed. Check the laws in your area before using any tricks that I or anyone else give you about correcting your credit or adjusting paperwork to qualify for a loan.

That said, it is also unfair for you to suffer a higher rate on a loan because of easily corrected, untrue, outdated, or miscalculated negative data the FI reads about you. Two different people with identical credit history and debt can have wildly different credit scores and get different rates based on those scores. Much of my advice deals with ways of correcting any mistaken bad impressions the FI may have of you and of legitimately improving your credit.

How Credit is Calculated

You can tell that someone has been around for a while if they still call credit scores TRWs. TRW (Thompson Ramo Wooldridge Inc.) renamed the portion of their aerospace company that dealt with credit reporting to Experian around 1996. Experian has two major competitors, Trans Union and Equifax. These companies determine whether a person has the ability to repay credit card debts, thus showing their credit worthiness. Their mathematical formula is based on statistical information about the behavior of those who don't pay their bills. They have studied and ranked the common danger signs of people who don't pay their credit cards and assign numerical values to different areas of each person's financial behavior. By adding up and comparing these numbers, they get a number declaring the odds that a person will pay his credit card bills. You can think of them as setting the gambling odds on whether you will pay your bills so that other companies know whether to bet on you. Although there are several ways to compute a credit score, all three major credit bureaus use calculations derived by FICO (Fair Isaac Company), which has spent 50 years studying spending habits and credit usage. A FICO score currently ranges from 300 to 850, with a higher score indicating a safer risk for the credit card company. The credit bureaus may call their scores by different names, but they use the same program. The formulas and programs are constantly being updated and may change without notice.

Some books and websites claim to know the math used to arrive at your credit score. Since the math has never been released and is constantly changing, I would put little faith in that information. I have even seen "credit repair" companies and loan brokers that misstate the possible high and low values of the FICO but still claim to know how it is figured out.

No one outside of the programmers at FICO knows the exact formula for each sub-category, but here is what FICO will publically state:

35% Payment History. Determined by the payment history on your credit card accounts, from Visa cards to department store and loans. The model assigns greater weight to recent missed payments than late payments years ago.

30% Outstanding Credit. Based on the amounts you owe creditors. This includes the total of what you owe on all your accounts and whether you carry an unpaid balance on certain accounts like credit cards.

15% Length of Time. Attributed to the length of time the applicant has been a credit user. The longer, the better, assuming you pay on time.

10% New Credit Loads. Based on whether you appear to be loading on new credit. In other words, have you been applying for and receiving new loans in recent months. High activity in this category will lower the score.

10% Mixed Credit Use. Governed by the types and "mix" of your credit use.

Slight errors in the recording of a person's credit usage can incorrectly lower that person's apparent credit worthiness. Also understand that the credit bureaus are playing the odds, so a small negative can trigger major damage to your rating.

Many people have horror stories about credit bureau errors, and I am among them. My FICO score was in the 800's: a great score. A doctor then miss-billed my medical insurance company, who in turn informed the doctor that the account number they billed did not exist. Without contacting me, the doctor's office gave the account to a collection company with an incorrect address for me. The collection company sent a letter to me at the incorrect address, which returned to them. The collection company reported to all three credit-reporting companies that I was a "Skip," meaning that I had moved to hide from my debts. Red lights must have been flashing, because the credit reporting bureaus sent notifications to all my credit cards that I was a "skip." The first I heard about all this was when I opened my mailbox to find it full of letters from all my credit card companies telling me they had canceled my cards due to credit risk. The cards I owed money on lowered my limits to the amounts due, leaving me no available credit. Because of this false report by a collection company, my FICO dropped to the 500's in three days! My frantic and threatening call to the collection company forced them to immediately reverse the false report, but, with my oldest cards canceling me and my available credit now equaling my amount due, FICO's formulas showed that I had no credit and deserved none. Because the credit cards had already readjusted, I could not convince the company to look at my history before the error, leaving me no easy or quick way to correct the problem. I eventually fixed it, of course, but it took a lot of effort over a period of months.

You don't need to understand FICO's calculations, but you do need to understand how they affect you. As you may have noticed, even outside of human error there are some problems with credit scores and what they are said to indicate, especially when it comes to buying houses. First, even if the program FICO uses works without error, it is based on paying credit cards, not home loans. Although there is some correlation between credit card payments and home loan payments, many people who are imperfect in paying their credit card debts are driven enough to keep their homes to maintain their loan payments. A financially stable person might procrastinate and pay his credit cards late, but his home loan would be direct withdrawal and never late.

There are worse effects of the fact that credit was not designed to evaluate property loans. A property buyer's worthiness should not change because he recently had more than one loan broker check his FICO score as he shopped for loans. Sadly, this is exactly what does happen. Too many recent inquiries can drop your FICO slightly.

Because we do not know the formulas, we never know exactly where we are being penalized. Although the bureaus will give you your credit score rather easily these days, your number tells you little about where you can improve. If people knew what looked bad, for instance what percentage of your available credit they would penalize you for being a few dollars over, it would be easier to stay within the guidelines. There is debate on this, however my experience making slight changes to someone's indebtedness has found that if you owe over 50% on your credit card, your FICO will drop. Less comprehensibly, it can also drop if you owe $0.00, because the company assumes you do not need credit. Rumor has it that having between 30% and 50% on each card gives the best rating.

Here is a real-life example of how credit scores can fail even the most responsible of us. A 60-year-old man with a paid-off home wanted to take out a home loan so he could put a down payment on a new home for his son. The man had plenty of assets like stocks, but he never had credit cards because he always paid in cash. He therefore had no credit history with credit cards. Having been responsible with his home payments throughout his life, he should have been a perfect candidate for finance. Were the FIs judging based on his real estate track record, a 60-year-old man who had never needed credit and had never defaulted on a debt, who wanted the money to help out his adult son, and who was asking for a LTV of only 20% should have qualified easily. But never having had a credit card meant his FICO was very low, and the FIs are so stuck on the FICO score that it was very hard for me to secure this worthy man a loan.

Improving credit scores
You should start looking into your credit score and getting ready three to six months before you find a property to buy. I am very serious: right after you decide to look for property is when you start dealing with your credit! Good credit makes it possible to get a better interest rate and fewer fees, and there are good and legal ways of improving your credit if you start early. An experienced loan broker (in hopes of eventually being used to find you a loan) will often be willing to run your credit score without charge, review it with you, and give tips on actions you can legally do that will positively affect your FICO score.

Add a child
An interesting way to give a quick jump to a credit rating is something I found by mistake years ago, and which I now hear it is done often. I had wanted to give one of my sons the right to use one of my credit cards and added him as an additional signer on the card. When I next checked his credit report, to my surprise, my son had my credit card listed on his record. Per the report, my 18-year-old had 20 years worth of excellent credit! I have heard recently of unscrupulous people offering to add strangers to their good cards for a fee. This is fraud. But someone with good credit adding a relative or business partner is legal and, in fact, the whole reason the cards have that option. Never add your child as a signer to a delinquent credit card, because the delinquency will show up on your child's record as well.

Moving debt
You can improve your score simply by moving your debt around. Owing over 50% of the available credit on any one card is said to "ding" your score, but it is also best to owe at least 25% of the limit on each card. By paying yourself with "convenience checks," you can pay an indebted card with a card on which you do not owe anything to improve your credit. Level out the percentages of the amounts owed to be under 50% on as many cards as you can.

Keep Old Accounts

People often get upset at their credit card companies and cancel their cards. However, the average length of time you have had your cards is one of the major factors FICO relies on. If you have had one card for 10 years and 2 other cards for a year, your average time per card is 4 years $(10 + 1 + 1 = 12 / 3 = 4)$. If, however you cancel the 10-year card, your average would be 1 year $(1 + 1 = 2 / 2 = 1)$.

Another reason not to cancel cards is the effect it has on the ratio of your total debt to your available credit. If you have three cards, each with a $5,000 limit, your total available credit is $15,000. If you owe a total of $5,000 spread out among the cards, you have used a third of your available credit ($5,000 / $15,000): exactly what the credit companies are looking for. If you cancel one of the cards, however, you only have $10,000 available credit but still owe $5,000. You have now used half of your available credit, and your FICO has dropped.

This is not to say you must never ever cancel. If one or more of your cards has hiked the interest very high, and when you call to ask them to lower it they refuse, you may need to replace that card. But only cancel one card at a time, and when you do, apply for a new one with better terms.

Get More Credit Cards
In the months right before you apply for a loan, you should make no new credit requests. However, before that time, it is wise to use credit to set yourself up for a higher FICO. By gaining more cards with higher limits, your overall debt-to-available-credit ratio will be lower. When you apply for a card, one of the factors credit card companies use to decide your limit is your income. When you fill out this form, do not be modest. The IRS is not going to double-check. The credit card companies cannot call your boss and check, since you may make money from side jobs. Be optimistic about how much you feel you will make the next year, and the credit companies will give you higher amounts on your cards.

Raise your credit limits
Sometimes a simple call to the credit card company will get them to raise your limit. This is great, because the percentage you owe decreases with a higher limit. If you owe $7,000 on a card which has a $10,000 limit, that's 70%. If they will raise your limit to $15,000, you will then owe less than 50% on the card, giving you a better FICO. This higher credit is not an excuse to spend more money! This is to create a larger margin

between your available credit and your debt.

Do not get store cards
Years ago, I was in Radio Shack buying about $50 worth of stuff. The cashier offered me $5 off if I applied for a credit card. I thought, "Sure, for a few bucks, what difference could it make?" A few weeks later, I received a $5,000 limit card that was only good at Radio Shack. I have no idea what I was supposed to buy for $5,000 at Radio Shack. But the card turned out to be worse than useless to me. Credit card companies decide your limit based on a combination of your income and your FICO, and they know how much available credit is on your other cards. I could no longer raise my credit limits on my Visa or MasterCard (which charged less monthly interest) because those companies would see the $5,000 and deduct it from what my max could be. Let's say, based on my income at the time, that I was credit worthy for $80,000 in credit cards. Let us also say that that I had three major cards worth $25,000 each, for a total of $75,000. Before my Radio Shack mistake, I could have called Visa and asked them to raise my limit from $25,000 to $30,000. Now, I couldn't. I had to go through the trouble of canceling that store card.

My first credit card was Sears, and I applied 6 times before they gave it to me with a limit of only $200. Store cards have typically bad interest rates and terms. You can never move money onto them, and many only work at the stores that issue them. The only reason I can think of to ever have one of those cards is if you are just starting to establish credit. Even then, if you get too many store cards, you'll never have the available credit to get a better card.

Debt Reorganization Companies
Watch out! There are a lot of companies that claim to have many different ways of helping you reorganize your bad credit. Many of these will leave you worse off than you were before. For example, there are companies that will offer you a loan for the value of all your other debts, but that loan will max out your credit limit and lower your score. Some companies negotiate with your creditors to lower either the debts or the interest rates on them, but this gets reported to the credit bureaus and tells them you can't handle your own finances, which lowers your score. It's unfortunate that FICO penalizes people for trying to get out of trouble. It's an error in logic, and maybe someday they'll fix it—but right now, most credit consolidating still harms your credit. Therefore,

before you let someone reorganize your credit, verify what they are doing and what effect it will have on your score.

Fixing incorrect data
There are, however, things you can do on your own that can help your score, and fixing any incorrect data is a great start.

The first thing you will need is a copy of your FICO score from all three credit bureaus. The law requires your score to be given to you once a year at no cost, and it will not count as a "ding" on your FICO. You can get your yearly free report from all three bureaus at https://www.annualcreditreport.com.

Some companies offer your credit information for a fee, but only recently have they started including your FICO score, and sometimes that is adjusted slightly differently than the FICO they will show the FI. Don't subscribe to a paid service that does not give you an accurate FICO. The benefit of using these companies is that their reports usually do not show up as inquiries against your account. The downside, and the reason many of them do it, is that they may sell your name to loan brokers that harass you because they know you are looking for a loan. If you are looking to buy property, however, contacting one of these companies may be worth it. Since some of them sell your information to advertisers, I recommend not giving them your phone number. Another option is to contact a real estate agent or loan broker because many of them will supply this information for free in the hope you will use their services. Others will help you if you reimburse them for the cost of the credit check, generally $10 to $25. One inquiry into your score should not lower your score much, if at all, and if you do it many months before you plan on getting a loan, the record will be gone before the FI runs your information.

A bad score can keep you from getting a good loan, a borderline score may or may not hurt you, and a good score is always better. The companies that say they can fix your credit vary hugely in their effectiveness and diligence, but most of what they do you can do on your own. Even if there are things they can do that you can't, if you do the parts you can do first, they'll finish the rest at a lower cost.

Once you have your credit report, you need to find and sort through all the strikes the credit bureaus claim they have against you. Even the true negatives can be worth contesting. Many companies have online forms to simplify this process. Some people prefer to write letters to all the credit reporting companies disagreeing with anything negative. However: do not accidentally complain to the wrong credit-reporting bureau about an item it did not report. You will be letting that bureau know new bad information. Only complain about the information it does know about, and do it succinctly. It is enough to state that you disagree; further ranting gets you nowhere. Write something like: "XYZ Collection Account 123456789 -- This information is not correct and should be removed." The person you direct your letter to simply enters it into a computer and makes no determination. The last thing you want to do is confuse the data entry worker.

The credit bureau will take that information and contact the company that gave it to them to verify it is correct. If the company verifies the information in a timely manner, then the information stays on your report. However, very often companies can't find the original debt, find that they are wrong, or are so over-loaded with complaints that they can't get the information back to the credit bureau in time. That information vanishes from your report, and your score improves.

Most reports of negative information cannot stay on your record for more than seven years (exceptions are bankruptcies and some government liens). Note that this is seven years from the time of the "last transaction." For example, let's say that in 2006 you defaulted on a $1,000 debt. In 2012, the collection company sends you a letter saying that they will reduce the amount to $900 if you simply send in $10. *Don't do it!* That $10 brings the debt back to life for 7 more years. Had you waited just one more year, the collection company would have had to remove the record. Making that payment means that the debt will follow you until 2019. When you are checking up on your bad reports, this is another thing you can look into. Let's say you went bad on a debt in 2006, but the company did not notify the collection company until 2008, and you have made no payments and charged no money on this account since 2006. They don't plan on taking it off until 2015 (2008 + seven years), but you can notify them that the last transaction was in 2006 and the record must be removed by 2013. In some cases you can write: "XYZ Collection Account 123456789 -- This information is not correct and MUST be removed because the last transaction was over seven years ago."

Sometimes a collection company will promise to remove negative information if you pay some or all of the debt. Do not believe them. They cannot legally offer to remove the bad reports if you pay because it is a form of extortion. Look carefully at the wording of the agreement: you may very likely find something negating the benefits they claim to offer. Often, they simply tell you they will do it but send you nothing in writing: again, don't believe them. On certain occasions, if there is a dispute and you can get in writing that ALL the information will be removed because it was "incorrectly submitted" and that you are making an "Accord and Satisfaction," there are agreements that can genuinely help you. However, if you are not careful, you will end up paying them all or most of what you owe and they will either record the payment as a transaction, showing you were late for seven more years, or record the unpaid reduced amount as a "write off" for seven more years, which is almost as bad as not having paid anything. In short, because of the way the system works, it can be better to ignore a bill than to do what seems like the responsible thing and have it haunt you for years.

After you have disputed your bad reports, the credit bureau will contact you concerning what, if any, of the negative information it removed. Write back about anything it did not remove with any legitimate dispute you have or any good arguments you can think of. Remember that anything you say can be used against you, so kept it short and factual. Often, the bureau doesn't have time to deal with you. Especially in cases where the debt was only late but eventually satisfied, the credit bureau may find it easier just to give in.

Now that you have done the easy work and perhaps made some major positive changes to your credit, if you still need to, you can go to the companies that fix credit. The cost will be lower, since they would have charged a lot to do what you already did. Try to find a company that charges based only on its successes so you can believe it will be aggressive.

11. Financing

Unless you are independently wealthy, you will probably need to obtain some financing to purchase your property. Maybe you are only buying raw land in cash and plan to improve it later with a house, but you will still need to borrow funds to build the house. Maybe you have a friend or family member that will be your "strawman" and take the loan out under his name. Even so, you will need to get the loan and handle the payments. Even if you are not particularly wealthy, there are options.

Whether you can get a loan, and on what terms, can determine whether you make a profit. You are not going through all the trouble of buying a property to make money for the FI. You want to make a profit, and the cost is lowest for you if you do so with the FI's help. It is therefore very important that you set yourself up far in advance to get the best deal. Know how to bargain for the best loan and understand the terms and the benefits. Know enough to be able to check whether they gave you what they promised.

First, we'll need to go over the terms and the process of acquiring a loan.

Loan Terms
We are moving now into more in-depth information. In the next chapter, we will go into creative financing: how to obtain property with little or nothing down. In order to understand that chapter, we will need to spend this one learning to speak the same language. There are a lot of terms in the finance world. You don't need to know the entire lingo, but you should know how to ask for what you want and how to get yourself the best deal. A lot of math goes into loans, so I will be doing a lot of calculations. You don't need to calculate anything yourself, and I'll explain all the figures I use. If math is not your strong suit, you can still get the gist of my meaning while skimming over the calculations.

Mortgages and Trust Deeds
Some very knowledgeable people in the real estate industry do not know the different between mortgages and trust deeds. Even some that do

know the difference (like me) tend to use the term "mortgage" for both terms, since both refer to security instruments for debt. Full books are written about these subjects, but you don't need to be an expert on them, even if you work in the mortgage industry.

What you need to know is that different states have different laws governing how mortgages work, and these differences become important when a person loses his home due to failure to pay off debt. In some states, the FI simply forecloses on the property by sending some papers to the homeowner, while in others it requires legal action. We will go into this in more detail later, but for now we will define the difference between the terms.

A **Mortgage** is really the property owner giving the Fee Simple of his property to the FI by a deed. The homeowner retains the right to occupy and use the land, unless he defaults on the debt. When the owner pays the loan in full, the FI gives back the property. Although the actual workings are a little different, picture William drawing up a deed stating: "To FI, but if I pay my bills in full, then back to me." If you do not pay your bills, the deed goes into effect and the FI takes the property. This raises the question of what happens if the homeowner still has equity in the property after the FI forecloses. Historically, the property owners were out of luck: they ran the risk, and they lost. Back then, a person could borrow $100,000 on a $500,000 farm and fail to pay it off, allowing the FI to activate the deed and own the farm in full. It was an easy system to abuse, and deceitful people loaned small sums of money and took valuable homes. It's a classic movie plot, where the damsel in distress must save the family ranch by getting that small amount of money to the evil banker by Friday—utterly impossible, unless someone could just win that pie-eating contest for the cash prize… Fortunately, most states have since put in a lot of safeguards to stop this practice. Most state statutes require the FI to auction the property to the highest bidder, and anything over the debt and costs owed will be given back to the owner.

A **Trust Deed** is a safeguard to keep some distance between the FI and the property owner. In this type of deed, a third person is brought in to hold the deed. The property owner gives the deed to a trusted business, and that business guarantees that everything will be done correctly. William says, "I give my property to Ted. If I don't pay FI, then Ted can sell my property and pay FI what I owe and give me what money is left.

If I pay back my debt to FI, then Ted will give me back the property." Here, when the property owner does not pay the $100,000 debt on a $500,000 home, Ted will put the property up for auction. Someone buys the property from Ted at $450,000, Ted pays the FI the $100,000 debt and any interest on that debt while the house was for sale, reimburses himself for the costs of selling the property, and gives what is left back to William.

Point
A point is equal to 1%. The term is generally used to describe the fee to obtain a loan. For example, a FI may charge two points of the loan amount to cover the expense of giving you the loan. There may be other operational fees such as possessing, but the point normally goes to the salesperson or the company profit.

Fixed Rate Mortgage (FRM)
This has to do with how much you will be charged for interest on your loan. The FI wants a guarantee of how much it will make from you each month if it helps you buy a home. It looks at what it costs to loan the money out, and then figures out what profit it wants to make based on the risk factors of your credit, the home, and other things, to come up with a fixed amount. For the whole term of the loan, with a FRM, you will pay the same amount. Unlike with the ARM (which adjusts to the market costs of borrowing the money to lend to you), the FI is stuck only making that much. It therefore picks a number that gives it room to make a higher initial profit.

You may hear about "a 30-year fixed rate of 7%." This means that for the next 30 years, you will always pay 7% on the loan. This protects you from a rising interest rate, which could be to your advantage 30 years down the road. However, most homes are resold within 8 to 10 years and are refinanced even more often, meaning that the FI gets its initial profits, and you never see the long-term ones. Especially if you are buying a home to flip (sell soon for a profit), over-paying now to insure a decent rate 30 years from now may not be beneficial.

Adjustable Rate Mortgage (ARM)
With this type of loan, the FI "ties" you to some index. What this means is that the FI figures out how much it costs it to borrow the money it will loan to you, then decides how much profit it will receive. FIs use different indexes to calculate this, which you don't need to know about.

What you need to know is that the FI is simply guaranteeing that it will make a percentage over its cost, and you run the risk of that cost going up over time. Because you are taking that risk, the FI offers you a lower interest rate. If you are planning to sell or refinance the property soon, the risk is not very high. There is a limit on how fast the indexes can go up, and sometimes they actually go down. Interestingly enough, when the FI knows the rate on an existing loan is about to go down, it will often call you to try to talk you into changing to a fixed rate.

Amortized
This means that the FI calculated how to make all of your payment amounts the same so that by the end of a set amount of time, you have paid everything in full. Let's say you take out a loan for $100,000 at 5% interest for 30 years. 5% of $100,000 is $5,000 interest per year. But the FI asks you to make monthly payments of $530, which is $6,360 per year. By doing this, you have reduced the amount you owe by $1,360 on the first year. Since you owe the FI a little less the next year, less of the money you pay goes to interest and more goes to lowering how much you owe. After 29 years, you will owe only $6,195, so only $165 goes to interest, and the rest goes to pay what you owe.

On practically all loans, you are allowed to pay more than the amount due, and even a slight overpayment will make a large difference in how long the loan takes to pay back. Using the above example, assume you overpaid by $123 each month ($653). You will have paid the debt in full in 20 years! Let's look at the math. $530 per month for 30 years means you paid a total of $190,800 to pay back the $100,000 to the FI. $653 per month for 20 years means you paid a total of $156,720 to pay back the $100,000 to the FI, a savings of $34,080. Sounds great? Not necessarily: if you were able to use that money to make over 5% interest each month, that would have been more profitable. Depending on your other investments and your income, you can determine whether overpaying on a loan benefits you.

Many financial advisors suggest that if you are paid on a payroll, make half your monthly payment every two weeks. Since the second half of each month will add less interest than the first, these early payments will take years off your loan. I recommend that you make your payments as early as possible. Most people wait until the due date to pay a bill, but because the FI calculates by the day, if you are dealing with high interest, paying a few days or weeks early will drastically reduce the debt.

Negative Amortization
This means that each month you are paying less interest than the FI is charging you, and that extra interest is being added on to your loan. Still using our example above, let's assume the FI allowed you to only pay $400 (not the fully amortized $530) per month on the $100,000 loan. At the end of the 30 years, you would still owe them much more than you borrowed.

This may sound horrible, but it has its uses and can be valuable where money is tight. If you plan on reselling the home in two years and are able to keep, fix up, and live in the home as it appreciates in value, you may be able to pay off the $100,000 when you sell the house. Maybe you feel that interest rates will decrease in a few years, and you simply want to save money until you refinance. Maybe you realize that your company increases your pay each year, so you plan to start over-paying the loan in the future.

Balloon
Strictly speaking, a balloon is any loan where the last payment is larger than the payments before. When we talked about a negative amortization loan, the loan amount was not being paid off, making the final payment larger than the previous monthly payments. A $100,000 loan could be figured out so that you only pay the interest each month and still owe exactly $100,000 at the end. Another way the FI could offer you a loan is a "30 year fixed loan at 5%, due in 20." What this means is that you pay the fully amortized $530 each month, but at the end of 20 years you need to pay off the rest of what you owe, which will be $50,230.

Direct lender
We have talked before about the relationship between FIs and loan brokers. A loan broker "wholesales" the loan to the FI in hopes of offering you a better deal. If a FI, such as a bank, loans directly to the general public, then that FI is a direct lender. Confusingly, sometimes a loan broker has either its own funds or a line of its own credit, loans to you from those funds (and therefore becomes the direct lender), then sells its portfolio wholesale to a FI. This may sound similar, but it can make a difference.

The bad news when the loan broker is the direct lender is that it will be more stringent in qualifying you because it doesn't want a loan it can't sell to the FI. The good news is that, since all the paperwork is done in the loan broker's office, it is often much faster. Also, because it sells its portfolio in bulk to the FI, it gets a better deal. If it passes some of those savings on to you, you get a better rate. The main reason loan brokers do this is simply advertising: if a loan broker can call itself a "direct lender," it sounds like a much bigger company.

Prepayment penalty

This is a fee the borrower must pay if he pays off his loan too soon. Although this sounds harsh, from the FI's perspective it is understandable. It would be unfair to the FI if it went through all the time and trouble of making you a loan, and then you refinanced before it made any interest. Prepayment penalty is a kind of insurance for the FI. Because it feels more secure in the money it gets from the deal, it will either lower your interest rate based on how long your prepayment penalty is, or else pay your loan broker "points" to help with your costs. Hopefully, your loan broker will pass these savings on to you. Because of prepayment penalties, many loan brokers will work at no cost to you if you are sure you will keep the property for years.

If you plan to keep the property to live in or rent, then you can use the length of the prepay to negotiate a better interest rate. If you plan to flip the property, pay the higher interest rate and avoid the prepay. By giving a little you can get a little, so it is better not to care about what you don't need in order to get more of what you do need.

When I was working as a loan broker, I got clients who wanted everything. They would ask for 100% LTV, no verification of documents, the lowest interest rate, no points or fees paid, and no prepayment penalty. Not only would no FI want to loan on this deal, but how was I supposed to get paid for my time? Shop for the best deal, but be reasonable in your demands. It's all a trade-off, and everything works on calculations. If something is not important to you, then give that up to better negotiate for what will help you more.

Private Mortgage Insurance (PMI)

Private Mortgage Insurance (PMI) is when you insure the FI in case you don't pay on your loan. FIs will start requiring this after your loan to value (LTV) has exceeded 80%. It can become expensive and, unlike interest paid on a loan, is normally not tax deductible. When you see a

100% financing deal, there will be PMI. I can't recall ever giving a client PMI because there is a way to get around the 80% plateau by using two loans that don't exceed 80%. Even 100% financing can be done this way. In the example below, we will use a 95% LTV simply because with 100% financing, the FI's risk factor makes the interest rate very high.

Let's say you buy a $500,000 home and ask for a 95% LTV. You will have a $475,000 loan at 8% interest of $3,371 per month and the PMI of $316, for a total of $3,687 a month.

On the other hand, you can get the same 95% LTV with one loan at 80% LTV ($400,000) at 7% interest, equaling $2,589 per month, and a second loan of 15% LTV ($75,000), at an interest rate of 9% for $580 a month, for a total of only $3,169. Plus, you can write off your taxes for the interest on both loans.

If you were unlucky enough to have received a PMI loan years ago on a property you own, you can notify the FI that you want an appraisal of your property. If the LTV is now less than 80% because of appreciation and the payments you have made, the FI will remove the PMI from your monthly expenses.

FI Requirements
We have talked about how the FI reviews the collateral you are putting up (the property) and then checks the character of the borrower (credit score). It also checks to make sure you have the ability to make your payments by looking into whether you make money, have money, and can feed yourself and still have money left to make the payments. Different FIs have different requirements to meet. There are legal ways to state some information to better fit their guidelines or explain away certain facts as exceptions. Remember, however, that it is fraud to lie to the FI, and I do not condone it.

Income
When the FIs review whether you qualify for a loan, they use **ratios**. They look at what percentage of your income would be spent on debts to see whether you have enough to live on and pay your mortgage at the same time. Each FI's requirement may be different, but if the FI intends to sell the debt to Freddie Mac or Fannie Mae, then the FI will use those government-sponsored agencies' current ratio requirements. Let's say your loan payment will be $1,500 per month, you need to pay $200 a

month for your credit cards, and the FI has (for example—this number can vary) a 40% Debt to Income Ratio. This means that the $1,700 you need to pay cannot be more than 40% of your gross income. In the above example, you would need to make $4,250 per month before taxes.

There are many ways to adjust this figure, and the easiest is to lower your other debts. Not all credit cards or debts require the same payment-to-debt-size ratio each month, because you can pay in full in different amounts of time. For example, say you have two different credit card debts, each for $5,000. One is fully amortized for 30 years and charges you $50 per month, while the other is based on 5 years and charges $110 per month. If the latter were based on 15 years, it would be $60 a month, which would look better for the ratios, though you'd need to watch out for what the interest rates would do to the long-term cost. But if, for instance, you have a car you're paying off at $110 a month for next five years, you could transfer that cost to a credit card where you pay $60 a month for the next 15 years. If you have cash available, pay off some debts that require high monthly payments. If you own a home you will be selling or refinancing to buy the new home, get a line of equity on the old house to pay off some credit cards. The FI's ratios do not take into account what will be paid off on the old home. I have had clients pay off their car loans to meet a ratio, giving them better interest rates.

Aging Reserves
The FI wants you to prove that it is your own money you are using to buy the home and that you will have some left over for unexpected expenses. There are a few reasons it requires this: it shows you have the ability to manage your funds, that you don't have an unseen loan on your credit report, and most important of all, it shows that if you lost the home you would be losing your own money, which is good motivation to pay your mortgage. The most common way for the FI to determine money is yours is by checking whether the money has been in the bank for a sufficient amount of time. This is called the aging requirement. The FI aging requirement is usually 3 to 6 months, so put the funds in your bank before that time. If you have not done this, there are a few ways to save the situation. With proper letters and documentation, many FIs will accept that a relative gifted you some amount of money. You can also prove the funds are yours if you can show that you sold a particular asset to acquire them: for example, if you can show you had stocks or a stamp collection that you sold for the down payment on the home. I have seen FIs take a simple hand-written bill of sale as evidence the homebuyer

had sold some valuable asset. Like adding a person to a credit card as we discussed above, I have heard of people being added on a bank account as a signer, which is sufficient to demonstrate that they had the required sum aged.

Employment
The FI wants to know that you really have a job or steady source of income. It looks not only at the amount you make but also at how reliable your income is. Maybe you just got a high-paying job last month, but have no prior history of making that much, or you just changed your line of work. The FI will be concerned because you may not be good at the job, or may hate it and quit, leaving you unemployed. The easiest way to prove income stability is by showing the FI two years of pay stubs from your employer. But not everyone has an employer that gives pay stubs. Maybe you make your money under the table (the FI is not the IRS and doesn't worry whether you pay your taxes), or else you have a business where the gross income legally handles many of your personal expenses.

There are many legal ways of getting around this requirement. Maybe you can show that you make regular deposits into your bank account sufficient to meet the ratio. You can also obtain a no or low document loan for higher interest (see next section) that bypasses the requirement. If you have a business, the FI may require proof that you have a city license.

No or Low Docs
Income, as we have discussed, can be a problem. Loans have been made on trust alone, but these are risky, and after the most recent real estate correction for over-inflation (caused by loans such as this), you may need to go to a private individual. However, the FIs really do want to loan you money, as this is how they make their profits. Even in housing markets like today's, some progressive programs will always be offered. The FIs have programs that "trust" you to tell them how much you make called "No or Low Docs." The idea is to help the self-employed person buy a home by not making them show documentation, but they make it easy to lie. (Note that I am not encouraging you to lie on your documentation.) Sure, they give you a slightly higher interest rate because you can't prove you have a job, but it may be the best way for some people to go. They may ask for some minor documentation, such as a city license to do work, active for at least one year. Still, anyone

planning ahead could have received a license a year ago and not used it, so the verification is not very strict. They may require you to show large amounts of money being passed through your checking account to demonstrate that you have a second business, but as they don't check where the money came from or went, receiving and paying back checks to a friend over a period of months or using no-fee convenience checks to accomplish the same thing on your own can meet this requirement.

As the disaster of the recent housing bubble demonstrated, however, just because you can convince someone to qualify you for a loan, it doesn't mean you *should*. The ratios required by the FIs protect them from defaulting homeowners, but they also protect you, the prospective homeowner, from taking on a greater financial burden than you can afford.

Interest Rate
We have touched on this before, but now that you have a better understanding of how the loan business works, let me spell out for you in more detail how the lender determines the terms of the rate you will receive. The lender or loan broker's representative gathers information about the borrower, including credit score, income, savings, and other factors that determine loan worthiness. No two people are alike, and the lender must look at each client separately. Loan brokers have been approved by different FIs to sell their loan programs, and try to find a program to meet each buyer's needs.

Let's take a closer look at the FIs' loan programs and how brokers get approval to sell them. FIs differ in what they require before their money can be loaned and may have several programs that each carry different requirements. Each FI faxes or emails its rate sheet to the brokers every morning. This is a list of the FI's loan programs and what constitutes an acceptable borrower. On the sheet is a chart stating what interest rate it will charge for each program and how much it will pay a broker for signing a borrower up for a particular program. For example, the institution says that for a buyer of a given credit-worthiness, it will loan money at 3 points over prime rate. However, if the broker can convince the buyer to pay interest at 3.5% over the prime rate, the FI will pay the broker 1 point on the amount of the loan as a bonus. If the borrower will agree to pay 4.5% over prime rate index, the broker will get paid 3% back from the amount of the loan. The FI offers other benefits to the broker if the borrower agrees to a longer prepayment penalty or other conditions. As you can see, although the broker seems to be working for you, the worse the loan he gets you to take, the better his profit. Even brokers who tell you they will charge you nothing for a loan can make quite a bit of money back from the FI by talking you into a very bad deal. Most loan brokers are honest and make their profits fairly, but you should know that two brokers could offer you different interest rates for the same program from the same FI. Shop around. You are the client and it is your money, and no broker should be upset if you investigate other prices and terms.

Unless the loan broker is a direct lender (direct lender profits cannot be seen), the amount of money he made on the deal will appear in the escrow's closing statements. A buyer can negotiate that amount and put it in writing. For example, if you are not a difficult client who causes the broker lots of trouble and extra paperwork, 2 points may be fair in your area. You could pay the loan broker 2 points of the loan amount yourself, and in return require that he get you a low interest rate where he makes nothing from the FI. Alternatively, you could pay the broker nothing yourself but require that he choose an interest rate where the FI pays him 2 points. Ask to see the rate sheet. If the loan broker is being honest, he should show it to you.

12. Creative Financing

Sometimes, no matter what he tries, a buyer can't get a loan. Maybe the buyer has no cash, had a recent bankruptcy, owns so many rental properties that he can't meet the ratios, or fails to qualify for any of a variety of other reasons. The buyer will need to use more imagination and sometimes take steps that will take a big chunk out of the profit. However, if the deal is profitable enough, the buyer may be able to lose some of it and still make money. Some of the ways buyers do this have major ethical or legal problems, but there are some cases where a buyer can find an ethical nothing-down deal if he can handle the payments, plans to flip the house, or can wait for the tax benefits or tenants to even out the costs.

We will now talk about a famous nothing down (none of your own money is invested) method of home buying that has been talked about since the 1980s. The easiest way to do a nothing down is to find a lender with a program that will loan you all the money you need to buy the property. However, this normally requires excellent credit and gives you a bad interest rate.

You should understand that unless you got a great deal on the house, you would be taking a monthly loss. Here is an example: You buy a home nothing down for $500,000 at an effective interest rate of 8% with monthly payments of $3,650. It is unlikely you can find a tenant to pay more than $2,500 per month for a $500,000 house, giving you an upfront loss of $1,150 per month. Figure in vacancy, taxes, and repairs, and you have an even larger loss. Your yearly loss in this example is $20,000 per year. Frightening? Not necessarily, when you figure that you had no money invested. The yearly cost is the investment you will eventually make into the property, just paid in installments rather than up front. After three years, you will have $60,000 invested, a lot of tax write-offs, $12,000 of the equity (deducted from your debt to the FI), and a home that has increased in value to maybe $630,000, which means you can increase the rent to $3,000 per month.

Hard Money

There are private individuals that have extra money to invest in people who do not have the ability to qualify for a loan from a FI. However, most of these lenders expect a large return on their investments. I have seen deals as bad as the lender charging 20% of the face value of the loan for his "origination fee," and then interest exceeding the legal limits. Using hard money is not the same as going to the "mob" for a loan, but it may not be far off. A hard money lender won't break your legs, but he might take your house with the interest and late fees. Using one is fine if it's the only way to get into the house, but only if you are 100% sure you can pay the money back in a short time.

Most loan brokers know someone that does hard money. Often, these hard money lenders do not allow the buyer a high LTV. There are many ways to finance creatively; try to avoid hard money lenders if you can.

Co-signer

A co-signer is a second person on a contract, who promises to pay the debt if the original signer fails to, like when you bought your first car and your parents promised to pay if you didn't. Some people think that having a friend sign on as a co-owner it is like a co-signer. Not really! Most FIs will look at both of your scores and use the lower one to decide whether you qualify. Sure, it could help with proving income and aged reserves if your co-owner is cash rich, but otherwise it does not do much good. Married couples where one spouse has a bad credit score sometimes have problems with this. By buying the property in the name of the person with good credit and listing the spouse as a paying tenant, they can get over this hump.

Straw man

A common strategy is the "straw man" or "straw purchase," so-called because the owner is in name only and could be pushed over like a bundle of straw to reveal the real owner. If you put your trusted uncle as the only owner, but you live in the house and make the payments, your uncle is the straw man. After a year or so, you can prove you have made all the payments from your own checking account and have your uncle give you the house when you refinance under your own name. The first FI got paid on time and never knew it was a straw man. It won't care after the fact, since someone responsible was making the payments. The second FI doesn't really care what you said in the past to a different FI. By paying on time for the past year, you've established your reputation to pay in the future.

Double Dipping

If you can qualify for one home but are trying to also acquire a rental property at around the same time, you may find that having the first home on your credit keeps you from qualifying for the second. But if you plan carefully so that both homes close around the same time, and you run your credit through two different FIs, you can qualify for both homes. The FIs can't see that you are buying the other house because it is not yet reflected on your credit. Of course, if they ask whether you are planning on buying something else, you must tell them, because lying on the application could be fraud.

Buy and Refinance

Like most creative financing, this is costly because you will be paying some fees twice, but it can solve many problems. Assume you find a $500,000 home that you can buy for $400,000. When the selling price and the price the home appraises at are different, the FI will calculate the LTV based on the lower of the two values, in this case the selling price. If you have little or no cash, you can use one of those 100% financing deals we talked about previously, with an 80% LTV ($320,000) from one FI and a second mortgage from a second lender at 20% LTV ($80,000) to come up with the needed $400,000. Then you will be stuck with two high monthly payments based on 100% financing. The way around this dilemma is to make sure the second loan has no prepayment penalty (so you can pay it off at anytime), even if you take a higher interest rate and fees to avoid it. You will want to pay off the $80,000, which is at a bad rate both because second mortgages carry higher interest rates and because of the lack of prepayment penalty. Quickly do cosmetic repairs or whatever the house needs to raise the appraisal to $500,000. Go to a new FI for a new second loan or a line of equity (a simpler form of a second mortgage that requires less paperwork and allows you to write checks against a line of credit). The home appraises at $500,000, so only having loans up to $400,000 will not break the 80% threshold for increased rates. You could get a loan large enough to pay off the bad loan, or else get a 90% loan to value, which will indebt you up to $450,000 but also put $50,000 into your pocket.

Credit card

By using the methods of improving credit we talked about, you can raise your credit limits. Get a credit card with no debt on it that sends you cash advance checks allowing you to spend up to your credit limit. Gather checks that charge either zero or low interest for 9 months to a year. Front (advance) yourself the value of your credit limit by writing a check to yourself and depositing it in a personal bank account. Less than a month later, have your credit report run by the loan company you plan on using. Because the increased debt will not yet show up to drop your credit score, you will get a good credit report, likely valid for the next three months. Start looking for a below-value property. When you find the property you want, contract to buy in 30 days. The FI requires you to have aged your money for at least 90 days (some require longer), but there are ways around this, as we discussed above, either with a letter declaring that someone gifted you the money, or by claiming to have sold something valuable you owned. For a limited period of time, your bank account shows the money, but your credit report does not show the loans. Thus, you had the money in the bank and the excellent credit to get a good and easy loan. After escrow closes and transfers the home to you, you can save money for 6 months to repair your finances. During those 6 months, you will be paying little or nothing on the down payment because of the attractive short term offers you received from the credit card companies for the credit checks, many of them at 0%. Since your home was undervalued, get a new appraisal and go to a different bank to obtain an equity loan (like a second mortgage) against the home, based on the higher value. Use that loan to pay off the credit cards before the companies raise the interest rates. You end up with 100% financing with good rates on a home you did not have the down payment to buy. The lender would likely consider this deceptive or maybe worse, so legally you would need your lender's approval to do this trick.

Seller Adjustments?
This is a strategy that used to work but no longer does, though many seasoned buyers still believe in it, and midnight infomercials still include it. About 20 years ago, a seller could pay a buyer to buy his home above the cost in order to show an inflated price so the FI would not see what LTV the buyer was really asking for. For example, if the home was listed at $400,000, the buyer would offer $500,000 if the seller would give the buyer a gift of $100,000. This way, the real price was $400,000, but the paperwork would reflect $500,000, and what the FI thought was 80% LTV would be for $400,000, the entire sales price. The buyer would get 100% financing at a rate the FI would have given to an 80% LTV. The FIs now check the escrow paperwork to verify that this is not happening. The appraiser would also very likely notice the inflated value, unless the

house was unusually difficult to appraise. You would have to really go out on a limb to try this type of deal now. For instance, the buyer could trust the seller to sneak him the cash afterwards, but the buyer has no recourse if the seller doesn't come through: you can't sue someone for failing to fulfill an illegal deal. I have heard of a buyer's relative acting as a straw man buyer who then flipped a double escrow to the real buyer with an inflated appraisal—but this is still fraud. Besides, if the profit appears larger, there will likely be tax repercussions to take away a big chunk of it.

Seller Carry Back

This can get a person a nothing down deal. We will again use the home for $500,000 as an example. Then we will take the widow from an earlier chapter who owns her home outright and just wants to move to where her children live. Buy the property at 80% LTV, but instead of the standard down payment, get a second loan from the widow for the remaining $100,000. This is called carry back. Assuming the widow can trust you to pay, everyone in the deal receives what he wants. You have gained a home for no cash. The widow has $400,000 cash from the bank, plus your repayment of her $100,000 over the next few years. The FI has a secure loan at 80% LTV. The problem you will need to get over is that since you can't show the bank you have any of your own money invested, it may jab you with a higher interest rate.

Inflated Appraisals?

One method people have used to convince a FI to loan at a higher LTV (usually in a refinance) is hiring an appraiser to over-value the property. This is illegal, and the FIs know to look for it. Appraisers must be approved by the FI, and the FIs share information with each other about any appraisers caught inflating estimates and refuse to use their services. It is, however, possible to talk to an appraiser about things he may have overlooked that would bump up the value of the subject property: "This house has an advanced security system!" or "The similar house down the street was sold cheaply because it was in bad condition at the time." Remember, however, that appraisers are not going to put themselves out of business so you can get a slightly better deal. The FIs will often check an appraiser's work with what is called a Desktop Appraisal (a simple computerized check of prices in the area) to see whether they will accept an appraisal.

Interesting story break. I had loan dropped on my desk where the home was appraised at $4,500,000, and the owners only wanted a 70% LTV ($3,375,000 loan). This seemed like a simple loan, but as I was about to sign it, I noticed in the paperwork that the appraiser had been paid $5,000 for his work! For a small home, $300 was the going price, and even for a multi-million-dollar home I couldn't see the price going higher than $1,500. Something was wrong, so I did my own investigation. The property was in a well-known, upper-class beach area, but up in a canyon, away from the water. It turned out that the appraiser had calculated based on homes right on the beach. I recalculated the value of the subject home compared to homes in the canyon and came up under $2,000,000. Checking when the owners had bought the property, I found they only bought it two months before at $1,750,000 with a nothing down deal. Had this loan gone through, the owners would have taken the money, never made a payment, lived in the house for free until it was foreclosed on, and then left the country with at least $1,625,000 in their pockets.

Phony Paperwork?
Creating fake paperwork is very illegal can get you years in prison. I list this here only for experts who need to know the kind of fraud they should watch out for. If I had allowed that canyon area deal I mentioned to go through my office, and the owners and appraiser had disappeared with the money, the FI would have come after me as a co-conspirator. I have had clients turn in pay stub copies for employment verification that had their names offset and in the wrong font on the slip. This means that they took someone else's pay stub and pasted their own names on top. Some more sophisticated fraudsters get their bank statements over the computer and use a program to go in and adjust the numbers before printing the documents. Although this may sound like a rare occurrence, I am pretty certain it is done often.

Conclusion

Now you know everything you <u>must</u> know before buying real estate. To fully understand any one part of real estate could take a lifetime of study, but only people who make a profession of teaching it need to know that much. Someone once asked me, "Why should I learn something when I can pay someone that already knows it?" It's true that you don't need to go to medical school to get a checkup. Likewise, allow your accountant to tell you the best tax advice for your situation, your attorney to handle evicting a bad tenant, a structural engineer to design a second story foundation, and whomever else you need for the expertise you require. You are the boss of your destiny, but don't try to micromanage.

What a buyer needs to know is how to think in terms of the concepts that make some deals work and others not work. My intent was not to cram in information you will never need or use, but to teach you what you need to understand to buy property wisely.

I am in favor of people owning and making money from property. But if you are going to go into this, have a plan before you start. Many people buy property in the hope that it will increase that 8% in value soon so they can use it to buy more property with the same estimated return on investment. Remember that while almost any 10-year period will show that 8% growth, the market fluctuates, and any given year can have less growth, or even a drop in price. In other words, never enter into a long-term investment if you can't afford the payments on your established income.

Don't let anyone deceive you: making money from real estate takes a lot of hard work. There is no mailing list you can sign up for that will cause people to start giving you money, and don't let the midnight infomercials tell you otherwise. Plan on spending a lot of time before you get any results. Study the areas where you want to buy and become an expert in the values, just as anyone should before making a big investment. Know how to approach people who may be willing to sell for under market value. Learn to find ways of solving sellers' problems to make it worthwhile to them to give you a good deal. Plan on many refusals before you nail a deal. Don't get stuck on a bad deal too long, hoping to make it better. Understand what goes on behind the scenes in the real estate industry and save all the money you can by being part of the process. Decide how best to use your property in order to make the best return on your investment. Money not spent is profit, so watch your expenses.

Most of all, hope for luck, but count on your skill.

#